*LEARNING THE POSSIBLE*

# *Learning the Possible*

## Mexican American Students Moving from the Margins of Life to New Ways of Being

REYNALDO REYES III

*With a foreword by Christian J. Faltis*

THE UNIVERSITY OF
ARIZONA PRESS
TUCSON

The University of Arizona Press
www.uapress.arizona.edu

Printed in the United States of America
21  20  19  18  17  16      7  6  5  4  3  2

ISBN-13: 978-0-8165-2126-5 (cloth)
ISBN-13: 978-0-8165-3560-6 (paper)

Cover design by Leigh McDonald
Cover photo by Aurelio Hernandez, Jr.

Publication of this book is made possible in part by the proceeds of a permanent
endowment created with the assistance of a Challenge Grant from the National
Endowment for the Humanities, a federal agency.

Library of Congress Cataloging-in-Publication Data
Reyes, Reynaldo, 1973–
    Learning the possible : Mexican American students moving from the
margins of life to new ways of being / Reynaldo Reyes III ; with a foreword
by Christian J. Faltis.
        pages cm
    Includes bibliographical references and index.
    ISBN 978-0-8165-2126-5 (cloth : alk. paper) 1. Mexican-American children—
Education. 2. Mexican-American youth—Education. 3. Mexican-American
students—Social conditions. I. Title.
    LC2682.R49 2013
    371.829'68073—dc23

                                                            2012036272

♾ This paper meets the requirements of ANSI/NISO Z39.48-1992 (Permanence
of Paper).

# Contents

# Illustrations

# *Foreword*

## Christian Faltis

THIS BOOK EXPLORES the experiences of five Mexican American students who develop emergent discourses (Gee, 1992) of community, resilience, and self-pride to navigate through the first year of college, a seemingly elusive goal at the outset. We learn how each student in the process of going to college gains an identity affiliation with what it means to be successful as a student, an identity shift that transforms them from marginalization to hopefulness and agency. This movement from the margins of a community of practice requires multiple adjustments in identity affiliation, practices, and allocation of time, energies, and focus. This book makes the shifts of five Mexican American students visible and accessible to a wide audience, showing through extensive cross-case analysis the power of community caring and individual growth over a period of one year.

The book resonates with me for personal and academic reasons. One of my first professional positions right out of college was as Program Coordinator for the Washington Neighborhood Center (WNC), in Sacramento, California, where I worked from 1973 to 1975. The WNC is a recreational and educational center for Mexican American and Chicano youth, many of whom were from backgrounds similar to those of Laura, Cristina, Maria, Luz, and Ruben, the students highlighted in this book. At that time, theoretical explanations for why Chicano youth did poorly in school, dropped out

of school, and rarely went on to college were based on blatantly racist accounts of inferior intellect among non-white children, and on
ideas about what it meant to be reared in poverty. At that time, Oscar
Lewis's the *Culture of Poverty* (1966) captured much attention as a
way of understanding the difficulties faced by children, principally
non-white children, who are socialized under conditions of poverty.
Their failures in school were largely a result of the cultural practices
that families living in poverty appeared to promote. In other words,
they were the victims of their own cultural practices; the school
system, the political legal system, racism, and the economic system
of domination and hegemony did not figure into the explanation.
Families and children raised in poverty were viewed through a deficit
lens, ultimately responsible for their own failures and marginality,
while the systemic, structural, and culturally dominant models were
absolved of their impact on the lives of poor, Mexican American children in the United States. I never bought into that view of children
and the culture of poverty, and I reject it vehemently today. In my
work with these youths at the WNC, I learned that the families had
myriad struggles, but more importantly I learned through my interactions with the schools these students attended that the schools
had little interest in making social and academic success a priority
for these students. There were no Mexican American teachers; the
school treated students as if their language and cultural practices, at
best, did not exist and, at worst, were unworthy of any attention
in the curriculum. The educational needs of Mexican American and
Chicano students were essentially disregarded.

Moving forward to the present, nearly a half century later, the
dominant paradigm that promotes a deficit model for explaining
school success and failure of Latino children remains intact. Today, I
teach in a university, working mainly with teachers to prepare them
to work with emergent bilingual students and immigrant communities. The dominant script has hardly changed since I entered the
profession as an assistant professor in 1983. Success still is invariably
defined as acculturation, by fixing the problem, the child's culture;
failure continues to be attributed to the problem as defined by the
dominant group: students clinging to "Mexican ways of being," to
using Spanish (poorly or bilingually), and to living in economically poor Mexican neighborhoods (where there are violent gangs).

Mexican immigrant students are schooled separately from English-speaking students in tracked programs with watered-down curricula, and the focus is on learning standard academic English (Gifford and Valdés, 2006). Sadly, many Chicano and Mexican American youth continue to do poorly in school on standardized tests, with inordinately high numbers of Mexican-origin children leaving school without graduating from high school, and relatively few continuing on to college (Gándara and Contreras, 2010). As was the case some 50 years ago, the majority of today's teachers have little or no knowledge of Mexican American language uses, family values, and community practices. And many continue to subscribe to a deficit model for explaining the failure of Mexican-origin students, fueled in part by the growing perception among the masses that Mexican immigrants and their children are an undesirable drain on society, and consequently unworthy of attention in schools (Faltis and Valdés, 2010).

This book presents an encouraging twofold counternarrative to this persistent perception. One is that Chicano youth from uneducated family backgrounds, despite having tremendous odds against them, can succeed in school and college when teachers and peers make concerted efforts to engage students in practices that bring their struggles and tension to light, and that enable students to create new affinity identities about being successful in school. The second counternarrative, more of a general theme than a particular focus, is that these youth are our future. Mexican American children are a large part of the United States population. We as a nation need to do a much better job of making sure that children like those presented in this book are more justly attended to during their K–12 educational experiences.

The first counternarrative is told through the theoretical lens of participating in a community of practice, a conceptual framework for understanding how members at the periphery of a community gain entrance to that community through identity formation and practice in ways of doing and being that are recognized as markers of legitimate membership of more seasoned members (Lave and Wenger, 1991). What Reyes presents in this book is legitimate peripheral participation in vivo, through a series of case studies of five Mexican American youth who attend a one-year college program called CAMP. In the book *Situated Learning* by Lave and Wenger (1991), none of the case studies used as evidence for how the theory of situated practice works in a community of practice is as complex as formal education. Reyes is insistent, and rightly so, that learning within a community of practice is messy and fraught with tension about identity formation, change, and transformation. The youths portrayed in this book each brought to the CAMP program a set of practices and experiences that, when enacted with other members of the community (peers and teachers), set into motion the key interactions needed for gaining fuller membership in the community of practice around being a college student in the CAMP program. Accordingly, while acknowledging the potency of past experiences (gang life, teenage pregnancy, extensive family duties, separate role relationships based on gender), Reyes makes a strong case for students' agency and empowerment to add new identities to those they relied on prior to entering the program. This is an important take-away from this book: marginalized students can be successful when the educational contexts support students' efforts to create identity affiliations as members in the community of practice. In this sense, it does "take a village to raise a child." To the extent the community recognizes the value of the new member for contributing to the community, and the new member recognizes the power that comes with participation in and new identity affiliations with the community of practice, successful learning will occur. As Reyes points out throughout the book, there will be tensions and struggles, and learning—joining the new community of practice—is complex, often accompanied by new obstacles to overcome. The youth he studies are what might be called "village-shy"; in their prior schooling experiences, the villages responsible for inviting them into school communities of practice essentially did not offer them the support and guidance they needed for membership.

This highly readable account of learning what is possible offers teacher educators, teachers, and educators a sophisticated and nuanced pedagogy of hope (Freire, 1995), predicated on the belief and commitments in practice (Faltis and Coulter, 2007) that when educators learn about the lived experiences of students through dialogue, and work together toward transforming reality, all sorts of good things can happen. The book also enriches our understanding of communities of practice, and the power of interaction, agency, and cultural pride for gaining access to new communities of practice.

It offers a rare and deep look into the lives of five Chicano youth and tells their stories through their own words, stories of struggle and accomplishment. In the end, I share Reyes's hope that all of us try to do better in education because so much is possible when we truly invest in the youth of today.

## References

Faltis, C., and Coulter, C. (2007). *Teaching English learners and immigrant students in secondary school settings*. New York, NY: Merrill/Prentice Hall.

Faltis, C., and Valdés, G. (Eds.) (2010). Education, immigrant students, refugee students, and English learners. *Yearbook of the National Society for the Study of Education*. New York, NY: Teachers College Press.

Freire, P. (1995). *Pedagogy of hope*. New York, NY: Continuum International.

Gándara, P., and Contreras, P. (2010). *The Latino education crisis: The consequences of failed social policies*. Cambridge, MA: Harvard University Press.

Gee, J. P. (1992). *The social mind: Language, ideology, and social practice*. New York, NY: Bergin and Garvey.

Gifford, B., and Valdés, G. (2006). The linguistic isolation of Hispanic students in California's public schools: The challenge of reintegration. *Yearbook of the National Society for the Study of Education*, 105(2), 125–154.

Lave, J., and Wenger, E. (1991). *Situated learning: Legitimate peripheral participation*. Cambridge: Cambridge University Press.

Lewis, O. (1966). *The culture of poverty*. Retrieved from http://lenguaix.pbworks.com/f/Culture+of+Poverty.pdf.

# Acknowledgments

FIRST AND FOREMOST, I would not have been able to finish this book without the encouragement, love, and support of my awesome wife, Lorie. She worked just as hard as I did to get this book done. Thank you for everything, Babe! And thank you to my wonderful children—Alexis, Jonah, and Mia—for being my daily inspirations to continue doing what I do.

I am so grateful to many people who played a part in the writing and completion of this book. First, thank you to everyone who participated in the study—the CAMP coordinator, CAMP counselor, recruiter, instructors, mentors—and especially to the CAMP students. I hope your story is told well here. Thank you so much to Char Ullman for reading the manuscript and providing such wonderful critique, suggestions, and feedback. I am fortunate to work with someone like you. Many thanks to Ben McDermott for his willingness to review the book manuscript on such short notice and to provide great feedback on specific ideas and details. Thank you, Chris Faltis, for your unwavering mentorship, guidance, and support. Sally Galman, I love the style, grace, and artistry you put into everything you do. Thank you for your feedback on parts of the manuscript, and for your encouragement. Thank you, Kathy Staudt, for your advice and words of wisdom. Thank you, JR, for your great work in capturing the right image for the cover of the book. Thanks to Joe Romero for being such a great friend and supporter in all that I've done since the sixth grade back in Big Piney, Wyoming. And thank you, Mom, Mario, and Dad. I am here because of you, and I love you for that.

Finally, thank you, God, for giving me the strength and courage to see this through and for making all of the people mentioned above, and so many others, a part of my existence. They all have had a part in shaping who I am and what I do today. And for that, I am so grateful.

*LEARNING THE POSSIBLE*

# 1

## *Introduction*

### Urgency of Incompleteness

> Hope is rooted in men's incompletion, from which they move out
> in constant search—a search which can be carried out only in com-
> munion with others.
> —Paulo Freire, *Pedagogy of the Oppressed*

THEY STILL HAVE HOPE. They are still there. We know they are,
but too many today choose to ignore them. They, the marginalized,[1]
are the students who have been discarded, forgotten, in the name
of everything in the history of our schools. Color. Language. Economics. Efficiency. High test scores. They still have hope that they
can have an experience that may change something about their lives,
their schooling, their learning. They still have hope that they can
make something of their lives. They just need that *right* experience.
Often it takes just one experience. Perhaps one book. Maybe one
person. One event. One chance at an opportunity. And such an experience may greatly change those who come from the margins of life.
Often, the change comes as the fruit of struggle for these individuals,
and new visions of what is possible emerge.

In successful education reform efforts, sometimes these experiences can be crafted by design in schools or programs, when coupled
with a sense of hope. And at the heart of these reform efforts are
the students and their experiences. In those reform efforts, learning

in various forms occurs, followed by stories. This book tells such stories. They are stories based on the study of experience, learning, and identity/ies of marginalized Mexican American[2] students in their first year of college through the College Assistance Migrant Program (CAMP). They talk of how this experience changed who they were and how they saw themselves as students. The CAMP experience provided them with opportunities to prove their abilities as students; to have the opportunity to practice that which is required to be a successful student; to see what was possible in their lives in a community with others who had the same aspirations of success. The CAMP experience was a chance at achieving academic and professional goals, and to be put on a path to get there. The first year of college through CAMP was redemption.

This book examines the student lives of Laura, Cristina, Luz, Maria, and Ruben,[3] each with his or her own unique struggles and successes in the first year of college through the CAMP program. CAMP, a federally funded, one-year scholarship, is designed to help college students from migrant and/or economically disadvantaged backgrounds, most of whom are of Mexican descent, succeed in their first year of college. CAMP's principal objective is to put the students on a trajectory toward eventual completion of a bachelor's degree. Each student entered the program impacted by a particular life situation going into their first year of college—the consequences of extremely low self-confidence; struggles with the English language; clashes between gender-role expectations and the desire to pursue an education; teenage motherhood; and a history of gang membership. Research shows that in the first year of college the daily situations and minor details of life often add up to larger issues and present overwhelming obstacles (Brooks and DuBois, 1995). For the CAMP students, the weight of the particular life experiences they took into their first year of college made academic success seem elusive, unattainable.

In the US schooling system, the student of Mexican descent is no stranger to adversity in life and learning. This Latina/o subpopulation continues to deal with the complexities and difficulties of poverty, peer pressure, crime, discrimination, language, and the like getting in the way of success in school (Donato, 1997; Gándara and Contreras, 2009; Moreno, 1999). Such issues are spilling over into the college-level experience for growing numbers of Mexican American students. The problem of noncompletion of two- and four-year degrees has become almost as pervasive as the high school dropout situation for students of Mexican descent. Although more Latina/o students than ever are enrolling in postsecondary institutions, in terms of completing a bachelor's degree they continue to be the least educated major racial or ethnic group (Fry, 2002, 2004, 2001i). In 2010, only 13 percent of 25-to-29-year-old Hispanics had completed at least a bachelor's degree, compared to 53 percent for non-Hispanic Asian young adults, 39 percent for white students, and 19 percent for non-Hispanic black students (National Center for Education Statistics, 2011).

Even with the guidance and support of the CAMP program, a history of academic underpreparation and living on the margins of society or within their own world of isolation was evident in how the CAMP students dealt with the minutiae of college life and expectations. Their marginalization not only impeded their social and educational mobility but created a continuous struggle with learning how to become successful students. But becoming a successful student is not solely an individual, isolated endeavor. Marginalized students are products of history, of their environments, of a schooling system built by others from dominant and hegemonic ideologies that are vastly different from those they are designed to teach. Our social and institutional structures continue to perpetuate failure for minoritized and marginalized student populations and label them as such throughout their entire schooling (Varenne and McDermott, 1998). And it is difficult for them to overcome such a stigma.

For many Latino students, no matter how weak or strong their academic preparation, numerous variables, such as cultural and social isolation, the effects of negative stereotypes, the consequences of low expectations from teachers and peers, and unsupportive educational environments, all affect performance and persistence in school (Oseguera, Locks, and Vega, 2009). These dynamics affect a student's ability to visualize success and completion, which ultimately is projected in and from his or her identity as a potentially successful student. The students highlighted in this book went into their first year of college through CAMP not having had the opportunity to firmly establish, learn, or engage in the practice of the identity of a successful student. For many marginalized Mexican-descent students, this process of learning how to be and enact the identity of a successful student is a constant source of tension, struggle, and frustration (Koyama and Gibson, 2007). But learning this identity of a successful student is paramount. Building on Wenger's (1998) belief that education should first be approached in terms of "identities and modes of belonging" and then as the acquisition of skills and knowledge (p. 263), I contend that an identity of a successful student for marginalized Mexican-descent students in today's schooling paradigm is vital and *the first building block* of academic engagement and positive performance at all levels of schooling. Academic and schooling success for many marginalized Mexican American students begins with and resonates from how they perceive themselves and their abilities, and how they enact those abilities. Learning is engagement. Engagement is identity. And identity is the foundation for academic success. If learning this identity does not happen, then academic success is rarely possible (Cummins, 2000).

But why *successful* student identity? How is this different from just student identity? Everyone is a student—of home, of school, of life. All students have and internalize an identity as a student. But for further learning, understanding, and empowerment to occur, the student identity must be and do more. And this is what we must be concerned about in today's schooling paradigm—marginalized students feel like they are *just students* in our schools. They simply exist. The marginalized do not feel like successful students. Or at least it is difficult for them to reach this place and sense of being. They are disengaged, disenfranchised, disillusioned. In what I explore here, the study of the marginalized learning a successful student identity is an examination of how we may give purpose to such students just existing in our schools. Looking at how a successful student identity is learned is looking at the source(s) of what drives a student's curiosity and passion in the educational endeavor, a sense of understanding one's role and potential within an educational space, but with a desire for growth, change, and empowerment. A successful student identity is the multiple connections to the curriculum, to words, to ideas, to people, and interactions with such people that bring to question relevance and existence in the schooling process. And learning a successful student identity is achieving a sense of self-understanding of what is possible in and out of school. This learning of a successful student identity is reaching a place of awareness of the actions, ways of being, skills, schooling knowledge, and empowerment required to be successful, and to feel and internalize what it is to be a successful student. It is a place of identity within the trajectory of school and schooling that fuels future efforts in learning. Moreover, the study of a successful student identity of the marginalized is aimed at further understanding the humanness of teaching and learning and its importance in creating formal and informal pedagogical structures that bring these students from the margins of life and school to learning new possibilities of the self.

When coming from the margins of school and life, learning a successful student identity is gaining a sense of empowerment and agency that fuels a trajectory in any formal or informal educational setting within a community. Throughout this process, there is a renewed and reemerging sense of self as a student that not only is learned in academic achievement but typically begins with, and is maintained by, what I call "key interactions" (discussed later in the book) with others in their schooling and cultural community. Key interactions help to build or rebuild a student identity that has been diminished by a history of subtractive schooling (Valenzuela, 1999), personal life struggles, the lack of supportive networks (Stanton-Salazar, 2001), and lack of access to communities that practice what it is to be a successful student. This identity is typically learned within a social context in which academic and schooling success is guided by a more knowledgeable other(s) (Vygotsky, 1978). This learning of identity is done in conjunction with those others who are also on the same trajectory toward learning how to be within that situated space and time and become for the future a successful student (Lave and Wenger, 1991; Wenger, 1998).

For decades research has illustrated how the condition of Mexican-descent students in our public schools reflects the enduring inability of the educational system to meet the needs of such students, get them to graduation, and adequately prepare them for higher education (Gándara and Contreras, 2009; Garcia, 2001; Matute-Bianchi, 1991; Romo and Falbo, 1996; Stanton-Salazar, 2001; Valencia, 2002; Valencia, Menchaca, and Donato, 2002; Valenzuela, 1999). The results of such a legacy of education for students of Mexican descent have created a system of socialization and internalization of being defective, unable, less than, and inferior. The cumulative effect of this history has made them feel, and see themselves, this way (McHatton, Zalaquett, and Cranson-Gingras, 2006; Urrieta, 2009). But this also has resulted in a broader deficit perspective of Mexican American students that reaches beyond classrooms walls (Valencia, 1997, 2002), and the perspective that Latinos do not know who they are, what they are doing, or how to exist within schools and society. As Urrieta (2009) points out, the Latino identity has been constructed by outsiders as existing in a crisis, when in reality schools create and have created and perpetuated the crisis of not knowing how to effectively work with Latino students.

At the college level, the complexities of the clash of sociopsychological and micro and macro societal and schooling structures influence the behaviors, the decision-making processes, and ultimately the self-concept (identity) of Latino students. Because of the history of deficit thinking woven into the structure of schools, Latinos often carry vulnerabilities with them to college. They are susceptible to the development of a negative self-concept. This translates to negative perceptions of the idea of college because of the students' sense of misplacement within the college structure and culture. They are uncomfortable in this new educational context. They are uncomfortable as students. The history of underrepresentation in college speaks to their social position, a constant reminder of the dissonance between the cultural expectations of college and their home culture (Hurtado, 2002; Oseguera, Locks, and Vega, 2009). Many students like those in CAMP envision a dream of college, but when they get there they may ask themselves, "Do I really belong here? Am I smart enough? Can I make it?"

For much of their lives, the students you will read about have existed in a state of struggle, sometimes hopelessness, and were too often relegated to the margins of school and society. As part of the educationally underprepared, they have existed in "both a site of possibility and vulnerability" (Rose, 2005, p. 247), having had few opportunities, for whatever reason, to realize aspirations of authentic learning, understanding of academics, and knowing how to do school with success as an outcome. They are out of high school—some graduates, others GED recipients. But they come to their first year of college through the CAMP program feeling incomplete.

This is not a study or evaluation of the CAMP program itself. It is a study of the student experience. It is a look at how students, individually and as a collective, engaged in the practice of learning a successful student identity through the CAMP community of practice. This study considers how curriculum and pedagogical designs that are integrated into programs like CAMP realize the nature of academic success beyond just academics, and the significance of human interaction and relationships in our schools. As such, the CAMP experience for students coming from marginalized life situations may help us understand the power of intervention and support mechanisms in teaching and learning grounded in such dynamics. This is a study and story of Mexican-descent students coming from the margins of life and school, and how they dealt with the tensions of learning and relearning the identity of a successful student through the CAMP community experience in their first year of college. This is a look at the socially constructed nature of possibility and hope.

## The College Assistance Migrant Program

The student experience studied and explored in this book took place in the first year of college through a program called the College Assistance Migrant Program (CAMP). Federally funded through the Office of Migrant Education, CAMP has existed since 1972 and is based at institutions of higher education across the United States; it is designed for students from migrant, agricultural, and/or economically disadvantaged backgrounds. For the first year of college, CAMP provides personal, financial, and academic assistance. Also, students are advised about how to acquire additional financial aid and information to help them in their transition to the second year of college. Financial assistance through the CAMP program may come in the form of tuition assistance, funds for books, and/or a monthly stipend. In some programs, limited financial assistance is available in the second year of college. The number of CAMP programs at colleges and universities varies from year to year, depending on federal funding. In 2005, there were 45 postsecondary institutions with CAMP programs, serving approximately 2,400 students (US Department of Education, 2005).

The CAMP program highlighted in this book took place at Next Step Community College (NSCC) in a small, rural Colorado town. The college itself was very small. It was one building, built on the outskirts of town on an open field in 1984. The building was three stories high. There was one central office where registration occurred, tuition was paid, and class schedules were picked up. There really was no student commons. The closest area resembling that was an open space on the first floor with round tables, chairs, and a few vending machines. There was one computer lab. Most classrooms in the building were large enough to accommodate long tables and 20-30 chairs. During class these tables and chairs were often grouped into semicircles, so that students could see one another during discussions.

The five CAMP students highlighted in this study were part of a larger cohort of students (n = 22). The CAMP office was in the student lounge, where the students congregated, studied, and met with CAMP counselors and the coordinator. Those who developed the CAMP program curriculum to be administered at NSCC seemed to understand their students well. The program was tailored to meet the social, cultural, personal, and educational needs of the participating students, which considered their schooling experiences and histories of various forms of marginalization. For example, understanding their marginalization, the CAMP coordinator, counselors, and instructors recognized that the students might benefit from taking courses together as a cohort. So courses were offered in a learning community format where a cohort of CAMP students took two linked courses (e.g., psychology and English) for one academic quarter. This allowed the students to begin school together as a cohort, which encouraged study groups and support for one another. There were also biweekly meetings with the program coordinator and other program administrators, who provided information on scholarship opportunities and financial aid, study tips, and time for students to discuss struggles and successes.

Support mechanisms were built into the design of the CAMP program. Participants engaged in a cyber mentor program in which mentors and role models from the community provided personal and academic support mostly via e-mail, but there were scheduled times throughout the academic year where CAMP mentees and their mentors met face-to-face. For example, a dinner organized at the beginning of the year allowed mentors and mentees to meet and get acquainted. CAMP staff and personnel were available to provide personal and academic advising on a daily basis. Because students were expected to maintain a 2.0 GPA, tutoring and academic supports were available when needed, either by tutors outside of the college or by other students within the CAMP program. If a student was unable to maintain this GPA, he or she was put on academic probation and required to attend tutoring sessions. To build camaraderie and trust, students participated in structured social gatherings and team-building events, such as ropes courses in their physical education class (also called Adventure Learning). These programmatic efforts were designed to create a community in which all of the students, as well as the instructors, counselors, and CAMP coordinator, were available to one another through the first-year college experience.

Because of the unique and varied needs of our marginalized student populations throughout the United States, pockets of intervention programs and schooling ideas such as CAMP are created. This, perhaps, can be seen either as a way to provide a much-needed service beyond the walls of a traditional school program and curriculum or as an indictment of our current school system and its inability to meet the needs of *all* students with the teachers and resources provided to them already. Nonetheless, I believe that CAMP is an example of a program that provides students like those you will read about here with another chance in their educational lives, to make up for what their PK–12 schooling and marginalization did not give them, or even took away from them.

When I encountered the CAMP program for the first time as a graduate student, I sensed that the program was providing a unique service for the students involved. Although the program itself was important, I wanted to know more about the CAMP students. I wanted to learn what and how the students actually experienced CAMP, and not necessarily by looking at the nuts and bolts of the CAMP program. By today's schooling standards, these students would be labeled "at-risk." Considering the students' marginalized experiences, I wanted to look at issues of personal, academic, and cultural tensions and (mis)understandings within new social and academic contexts and influences on teaching and learning, and how all of these influenced their "student identity." More specifically, I wanted to see if and how students from the margins of school and life could use this experience to learn to become successful students over the course of one academic year.

## The Study: Methodology and the Personal

As a researcher grounded in qualitative methodology with an emphasis on ethnographic methods, I asked the larger research question: What impact does participation in a first-year retention and support college scholarship program have on situationally marginalized Mexican-descent students and their learning to become successful students? From this main research question I developed additional research questions that would help me to glean a sense of (1) the sociohistorical context of schooling based on looking at who the students were from narratives of their past and present experiences; (2) how they understood and reacted to the world of college as mediated by CAMP and what role they thought the CAMP experience played in their lives as developing students; (3) how they individually performed in the program—academically, personally, and socially; and, finally, (4) insight into the resultant aspirations, struggles, and learning that reflected new understandings of themselves as students from the various perspectives of those involved (i.e., students, instructors, CAMP counselors, the CAMP coordinator, and researcher).

The study took place in the 2002–2003 academic year. I conducted a qualitative case study using ethnographic methods, such as interviews and field notes from participant observation, in which I immersed myself in the culture and practice of the program (Creswell, 2007). This was a case study of the students as a group, and as five individuals (Merriam, 1988, 1998; Stake, 1995). I also used a narrative inquiry approach, which uses the story of experience from the participants as part of understanding their historical, personal, and schooling perspectives, processes, and trajectories (Clandinin and Connelly, 2000). Data sources were from field notes; structured and unstructured interviews of students, teachers, and CAMP staff;

student journals with researcher-elicited questions; audio-tape recordings of classroom interactions, meetings, and informal talks in the hallways or in classrooms before class started; video footage; and documents such as transcripts, letters, and e-mail correspondence.

Throughout this book, sources and analyses of data are triangulated to provide a fuller picture of the dynamics and context in which the students participated and experienced. For example, when looking at how the students changed after their experience in college through CAMP, the analyzed data come not just from interviews with the students, but from interviews with the CAMP coordinator, counselor, and recruiter, and from instructors. I have also included reconstructed field notes throughout to give context to a student experience that reflects the examination of a particular phenomenon. I interviewed the students four times: three to four months after the beginning of the academic year (to allow time for the students to internalize their experiences), in the middle of the academic year, at the end of the academic year, and at the beginning of the second academic year (to have allowed students time to reflect on their CAMP experience after they finished the program).

I went into this study grounded in a number of my own histories and identities of which, at the time of this research, I was not quite aware. But now in reflecting on the beginning and end to this study, I realize that a number of unseen motivations drove my inquiry. First, from the perspective of a researcher, my role in this study was as a participant-observer, which allowed me to participate in various activities throughout the academic year while being able to record what I saw and experienced. In this role, I sometimes helped students with their schoolwork, participated in Adventure Learning games, grilled hamburgers at a cookout, helped in purchasing needed school supplies, assisted with a scholarship application, or just hung out. As a reform-minded educator, I went into this study seeking answers about the role of programs in the intervention and retention of marginalized Mexican-descent student populations. Being of Mexican descent myself grounded me in this search for such answers. But I also come from an extended family of those who, like the students in this study, were marginalized in some way.

My mother was a child migrant worker. She lived in poverty, dropped out of high school in the tenth grade, married at 15, gave birth to me at 17. My father was an alcoholic and a drug user. My mother divorced him when I was around three years old. But I don't think he knew love from his own father, my *abuelo*. I don't think his father knew how to be a father, but only in the sense of being a "provider" by going to work, earning a paycheck. And his mother, my *abuela,* lived in a *machista* world in which she essentially lived to serve my abuelo and her sons. But they did not respect her. Yet she knew how to care and love. Many of my cousins dropped out of high school, were teen mothers or fathers, and, at some point in their young lives, lived on welfare, in government housing, or on some sort of government assistance.

I may not have experienced marginalization like my family, but their experiences have always been with me—personally, socially, culturally, educationally, linguistically. Because they are family, I lived and learned their marginalization *de aquí*—from here—a space where I have lived sheltered but still know sadness, struggle, and possibility by being the product of history and present consciousness of the tragedy of marginalization of others. Their experiences guided my schooling because I knew I did not want to do what they did. The memory of my marginalized family whispered influences on many life decisions because I knew my path had to be different from theirs. And they contributed to my identity as a researcher and to the questions I asked entering this study, because I wanted to know more about the marginalized and if it were possible to bring them back from those margins of school and life and to a place where they can experience something better. Perhaps, in doing this study, I was vicariously seeking a hope for my family of the past, but an elusive yet possible hope that may be found in the CAMP student experience.

## Conceptual Framework of the CAMP Student Experience

### Identity, Learning Identity, and Community of Practice

Rooted in the work of Vygotsky (1978) and the sociocultural nature of teaching and learning, this study considers how a student's surroundings and interactions with others in those surroundings socially and culturally construct what the student learns and becomes in that learning. Specifically, I look at the learning and identity development that occurs in the experience(s) of practice and movement from a marginal existence as a student in the first year of college through the CAMP community to a more enabled participant. The principal concepts that guide this study are identity, the learning of identity through peripheral participation, and the role(s) that the CAMP program community of practice and experience has on changing and evolving identities as successful students (Lave and Wenger, 1991; Wenger, 1998).

In this context, identity is the result of practicing what it is to be a successful student. A successful student identity is moving from a novice, peripheral (marginal) position within a particular socioeducational context to a more knowledgeable, perhaps even an expert, individual. But this identity is not a finished product. Its development and emergence is fluid. Continuous. Evolving. Incomplete. The CAMP scholarship and program gave the students the entry and opportunity to engage in this practice of becoming. While learning is the practice of participation and movement toward a particular target learning goal, learning also occurs simultaneously while people are engaged in the practice. Learning and identity are partly the acquisition of skills, knowledge, and understanding, which translate to their enactment in everyday practice. In this view of learning, one becomes what one is learning, and one learns as one is becoming (Lave and Wenger, 1991). Because identities "must be able to absorb our new perspectives and make them a part of who we are" (Wenger, 1998, p. 217), communities of practice that allow entry to the marginalized and provide legitimacy to such participants can provide a place for this process to occur.

This learning, and the learning of identity, occurs within a community of practice in which members, in this case CAMP students, have been given legitimacy through access and opportunities to practice college (Lave and Wenger, 1991; Wenger, 1998). The actual encounter with a new social and cultural world in which students navigate and engage through practice toward a particular learning goal begins to shape who and what they are. Learning to be and become a successful student and taking on an identity as a successful student emerge from experiences and interactions with the people around them, in this community that practices that which is to be learned. But to learn these new identities, one must gain entry into a community of practice (Lave and Wenger, 1991). Once they have gained membership into this community of practice, novices (in this case, the CAMP students) are taught or apprenticed by more knowledgeable others or experienced practitioners. But in this framework for understanding learning, the curriculum and that which is to be learned is the community of practice itself (Wenger, 1998). And because the entire community is engaged in some facet of interactional dynamics that occur within the trajectory toward a common learning goal, they influence new members of this community to move and progress from peripheral abilities and involvement to being a more knowledgeable and empowered participant. Participants are given legitimacy with their access to the community of practice and allowed to move beyond their peripheral or marginalized spaces in their interactions and learning with others. Knowledge, awareness, and understanding are not only acquired, created, and re-created but are projected in practice and one's newly forming and formed identity (Wenger, 1998).

## Tension and Boundaries in Communities of Practice

An identity also is the base from which an individual makes choices about life paths when encountering new worlds, and is the principal means by which one reacts to and interacts with the individuals within them (Holland, Lachicotte, Skinner, and Cain, 1998). But, of course, the learning of new identities does not occur without problems on these life paths. The formation of an identity(ies) must be grounded in an understanding of the self and how that self manages the conflict and tensions that arise in the interactional dynamics that occur within social and cultural contexts of learning (Josselson, 1994). Life paths lead to these new contexts, new worlds. And there are boundaries between these worlds of communities of practice. These boundaries define communities and the engagement occurring within, a sign of depth of learning (Wenger, 1998). As such, the base of a student identity positions an individual to navigate the intricacies of the histories, politics, economics, ideologies, discourses, and multiple pedagogies of schools. For marginalized Mexican American students, a successful student identity is not only the starting point of academic, literate, cultural, social, and personal engagement with school and its participants; it is the ability to manage conflicts of self that occur in the negotiation of the complexities of schooling life. These complexities often occur for marginalized students on the boundaries between communities of practice. Being within and navigating through the boundaries between communities of practice, Wenger (1998) calls multimembership. He considers this a place and movement to explore the possibilities in creating new knowledge, understandings, tensions—and power—of identities between these communities.

To alleviate the stresses of movement and practice of identity within and between the boundaries of communities of practice, students in schools today must be more than members of a class or community; they must actually feel accepted and sense that they belong (Osterman, 2000). This sense of belonging within communities of practice in classrooms is created in the interactions between teachers and students, students and students, and students and the words, ideas, and discourses that emanate from the world around them. Within a community of practice, interactional dynamics that are created in relationships are not only key to learning and the learning of identity. They must also lead to the shared understanding and use of social, peer, and cultural capital that result in academic success (Gibson, Gándara, and Koyama, 2004; Stanton-Salazar, 1997, 2001; Valenzuela, 1999). That is, these types of capital—interrelational and humanistic currencies and resources grounded in a cultural discourse of understanding and support of what is needed to do well in school—reflect a power in what is often immediately intangible but eventually seen through successful schooling.

Although the relationships and interactions that occur within a community of practice define a person, conversely the person in practice also defines the dynamics of the relationships. As such, this system of relations within a community of practice is a negotiation of learning, empowerment, and new ways of being (Lave and Wenger, 1991). There is tension, but it is necessary because it reflects movement from a peripheral space in the community of practice and how that movement is changing one's identity. There will always be tension in movement, change, and learning of an identity that is projected to the outside world and practiced with those in it. For the marginalized student, the negotiation of this tension is an integral part of the process of utilizing agency with his or her membership in the community of practice, formation of his or her new identity/ies, and the learning that is a part of becoming.

## Learning, Transformation, and Empowerment in Communities of Practice

Learning a student identity in a community of practice is multidimensional and constitutes, indeed goes beyond, the acquisition of skills, knowledge, literacies, and academics. Learning is transformation. In this sense, learning changes who one is and what one does as one interacts with others and their words, ideas, and actions within a community that is anchored by an alignment toward imagining possibility (Wenger, 1998). In the context of school, learning as a student is a constant rearticulation and reformulation of the self within and through the dynamics of school and classroom interactions. In this process of change and evolution of student identity, there is a constant vision of what is possible in their practice, vital to realizing transformation. In the CAMP community of practice, a vision of students being successful anchors the practices of all those involved.

For marginalized students, learning identity is also a tension of desire for advancement from their marginal space in school, life, and society toward membership in a community that contributes to their agency. Because once they have gained membership, their aspirations attempt to align with particular practices that will help them achieve their movement. They can then practice a skill, learn, fail, learn again, and attempt to learn the intricacies of practice that move them toward understanding, toward a new way of being. In Lave and Wenger's concept of learning (1991), engagement in the practice of learning new ways of being puts students in a position to advance beyond peripheral participation spaces, that is, in the case of the CAMP students, somewhere beyond their marginalized existences grounded in new choices made in their new practice(s).

The teachers or more knowledgeable others within a community of practice are vital in the creation and maintenance of a trajectory of learning, to apprentice a participant (student) from the site of his or her marginalization into a new movement, new direction in learning. Because learning in this sense is a broader social endeavor and creation of a path to new possibilities, powerful teachers become an invested part of the effective incorporation of a student's history and present skills while managing the tensions that arise in the trajectory of learning within the present (Wenger, 1998). Such teachers know how to mediate the tensions of the skills, knowledge, and new identities emerging as learning occurs. For example, consider a teacher of a marginalized student who is behind grade level because of a history of being "passed" through the system. This teacher may effectively engage the student academically by teaching her at her level of learning within her zone of proximal development (Vygotsky, 1978). In this meeting of past, present, and future practice of learning and identity, there is the history of academic and schooling marginalization coming from one community of practice to continued marginalization in another until the teacher has effectively taught and apprenticed this student to be at the grade level where she should be. Of course, this practice and pedagogy requires innovative manipulation of time, space, and curriculum that only the best and most passionate educators within a community of practice possess. Although there is risk involved in this teaching, teachers feel empowered enough to control their pedagogy for the marginalized in this manner. And this teacher empowerment often translates to student empowerment.

## Usefulness of the Conceptual Framework

The conceptual framework of communities of practice, and the learning of identity through practice, offers a persuasive way to look at how the students experienced learning in their first year of college through the CAMP program. The way that Lave and Wenger (1991) and Wenger (1998) look at learning as practice and movement toward a new space and emergence of identity presents a pedagogical approach for addressing the educational needs of the marginalized. One key aspect is the notion of *movement* for the marginalized. Movement from a marginalized position as a student is not only symbolic but actual when considering the newly learned, acquired, and empowered skills, knowledge, sensibilities, and identity formed after such movement along a trajectory toward learning how to be a successful student. For example, a high school student who is an English learner in a mainstream classroom has never had the opportunity to engage in small-group discussions with native English-speakers in a classroom to practice both social and academic English. She has been marginalized within classroom communities of practice in the learning of social and academic language related to the content area. But now that she, the English learner, is in a classroom with a teacher who has granted the student access to this new community of practice, she has the opportunity to move from her linguistically and academically marginalized position into one in which she may engage in the practice of language, academic, and content-area learning with the others in the community. In this movement from a marginalized position for the English learner looking from the outside of the community of practice, there is learning, but it does not come easy in those transitions within and between boundaries of nonpractice and practice.

Jiménez (2005), in her study of a Chicana writing group, recognized the tension in the movement of identity of one participant, Janet, in her writing community of practice. Within the writing process and discussion of this process with others, Janet revealed the struggles of immigrating from Chile to Canada. She realized how she was a member of several communities of practice, and that she moved from one to the other in her experiences as an immigrant. She found that movement between communities of practice is an emotional process. Knowledge and insight acquired in a new community of practice moving from another community of practice are gained at the expense of emotional eruption in the recollection of identity in history and the transition to the present. Similar to what Britzman (1998) explores in the psychological losses in the process of education, the movement incurred through identity transformation, in this case, was an experience of both emotional turmoil and new understandings. Still, something is learned in this process. This book explores this learning in the midst of intertwining experiences of the personal, social, emotional, historical, and academic.

The CAMP students entered this new chapter of their schooling still in their marginalized existences, their lives laden with memories of struggle, tension, and defeat as recent and not-so-recent high school students. The concepts of the social practice of learning and identity as learning, and these occurring in a community of practice, present a way to look at what is possible based on the human interactional dynamics of student experience in a program like CAMP. These understandings of teaching and learning remind us again of the importance of the human aspect of education, and the important role(s) that emotion, compassion, understanding, and empowerment play in the lived realities of marginalized students. This way of looking at learning presents us with other pedagogical possibilities beyond the status quo in the education of marginalized Mexican American students.

## What Is Possible?

In my teaching today, I often present to my students, who are future teachers, the question *What is possible?* I present this question in the context of the problems and complexities occurring in our society, schools, teaching, learning, and their future roles and identities as teachers. I ask this question when discussing teaching solutions for students from marginalized communities, many of them migrant farm workers who travel within the United States looking for work, immigrants from other lands, and those living in poverty, many learning English as a second language. I ask this question because I don't believe that we ask it enough in education circles. Or we may ask it, but we do not explore those possibilities. Or we may explore the possibilities, but we do not act. We may act, but the action soon dies.

Research often shows what is possible (Bempechat, 1998; Conchas, 2001; Faltis and Arias, 2007; Fashola and Slavin, 2001; Fránquiz and Salazar, 2004; Gándara, 2002; Gibson, Gándara, and Koyama, 2004; Mendiola, Watt, and Huerta, 2010; Rendón, 1994; R. Reyes, 2007; Rose, 2006; Salinas and Reyes, 2004; Slavin and Calderón 2001). I believe educational researchers, including myself, deeply yearn for the radical change of our education system. After immersing themselves in their research and seeing their findings, they can taste the possibilities of innovation, creativity, reform, and praxis. Sometimes researchers are privy to the results of praxis in schools or classrooms—action based on reflecting on what happens in the world(s) of schooling, and then reflecting on that action—resulting in change in individuals and communities (Freire, 1970). Education researchers have reached a new understanding of what is possible in our public schools. Yet most teachers in the public schools, those who need to see, understand, and implement these possibilities the most, rarely see this research, its power, and its potential. But they are not to blame. They may see bits of some important studies in a professional development workshop or a course. They may hear sound bites of the latest trend in teaching based on some findings. They may even get a graduate degree. But, often, it is not enough to reflect true change, reform, and revolution in the schools on a grand scale. It does not reach enough teachers, and ultimately the students. There are many fascinating studies being done in education research, with powerful findings that address the question "What is possible?" in education reform. But, unfortunately, educational researchers most often just end up reading each other's work.

Many, many teachers practice the possible. Unfortunately, this practice is often short-lived for a great many of them. Maybe it is too hard to implement. Perhaps it is just too exhausting to be innovative and creative. Or maybe they do not have the systemic support to engage in the possible in their pedagogy. Anecdotally, I know very well of these systemic roadblocks in implementing and practicing "what is possible" for teachers. In consulting with and having local teachers in many of my classes, I hear it all the time. But their hesitance is grounded in fear: fear of being discovered by their district administrators or being exposed by the "teaching police" for straying from the prescribed curriculum; fear of being blamed for not dedicating enough time to a particular math lesson or spending too much time on that vocabulary review. *Move on to the next lesson! If you don't like it, then I'll replace you with a teacher who will do what I tell them to do!* These are true echoes of their superintendents' voices driving their pedagogy. The reality is that not enough districts and schools with significant marginalized student populations attempt to answer the question of what is possible when considering program designs, curriculum, the roles of high-stakes standardized tests in their schools, and their impact on teachers, students, and the community. Too much fear.

This book looks back at what I found in this study of the student experience in the College Assistance Migrant Program and explores the question "What is possible?" in teaching and learning with the marginalized. With CAMP students having a nationwide continuation rate of 81 percent to the second year of college (Willison and Jang, 2009), compared to a national continuation rate of 66 percent for all students at all postsecondary institution types (ACT Educational Services, 2008), the CAMP program experience was something calling to be examined. With such students who come from the margins of life and school, how is it that so many go on to the second year of college? In studying the CAMP student experience, I wanted to see what was possible in *just one academic year*. What would the students learn? How much impact could this learning in a community with others really have on their learning? Their perseverance? Their resilience? Is it possible for these students to learn such a new sense of their identity and place in an academic trajectory that it can be seen in the way they present themselves to others, in their practice, in their stories, and in their grades?

The CAMP students participating in the program were actively seeking to make a change in their lives, in this case, by pursuing higher education, and enduring the hardship that typically goes along with pursuing it—getting to class; working long hours and trying to find time to study; pressures from friends, family, or lovers; and the like. These students were not forced to attend college. They attended college to have a chance at changing some aspect of their lives and their future, enacting their agency within a schooling experience in a program whose philosophy, design, and people further enabled and fed this agency. The CAMP opportunity was another chance, because for the marginalized student "desire depends on opportunity to be realized" (Rose, 2005, p. 247). These students entered a physically, emotionally, and intellectually challenging experience that pushed them beyond what society had expected of them. They practiced something beyond what many of them and their families had expected—beyond their present contentment, and beyond perhaps what many of these students may have seen at one point as their lot in life.

Knowing what is possible first comes with the ability to see it within. Sometimes this can be called hope. But this hope in schools—and the resultant individual aspirations for academic success—are also influenced by larger social structures beyond the self (Gibson and Ogbu, 1991; Matute-Bianchi, 1991, 2008; Ogbu and Simons, 1998; Weis, 2008). Hope is extinguished or fueled by one's environment, the people within it, and the interactions that occur therein. Hope comes from that outside the self which feeds the roots of ideas, stories, history, agency, and the identity of a new and possible self. Being hopeful is being active in that pursuit. And hope or hopelessness is projected through one's identity—how one sees oneself and is seen by the world. But identity is learned. And if identity for the marginalized can be learned, then so can hope. But, as Freire (2004) implores, "hope needs practice in order to become historical concreteness" (p. 2). Anchored in the hope to be good at school and to pursue a credential that will provide better opportunities in life, the CAMP students engage in that practice of what is possible, what can be real. This book looks closer at the learning, practice, and pursuit of hope.

In spite of the history of educational neglect and marginalization of Mexican American students in the United States, many still overcome their plight and succeed in school and beyond. This success is often driven by hope, but in settings that fuel this hope. Educators, reformers, and problem solvers of today's schooling for students like those who come into the CAMP program must consider the power and potential of how we design positive and powerful teaching and learning experiences and contexts that can help create hope for those who may have lost it. Because "hopelessness is a form of silence, of denying the world and fleeing from it" (Freire, 1970, p. 91), educators must be concerned that marginalized student populations live in some form of silence already. We must recognize that this silence may diminish what they see as possible and take away from an identity of a potentially successful student within the world of schools and schooling.

If there are marginalized students with agency and resiliency who can be successful in adverse social and schooling situations, can we imagine the greater possibilities for such students who are in supportive and positive schooling environments? This book is intended to provide insight into the experiences of five marginalized Mexican American students in their first year of college, mediated through one such supportive environment—the College Assistance Migrant

Program. I will show how and what the students learned from the interactions and relationships with those within the CAMP community while navigating the new world of college, and how such knowledge translated into new ways of being, a sense of hope, and a glimpse at what is possible.

## Notes

1. When describing students as marginalized, I am speaking of societal, economic, cultural, personal, ideological, or pedagogical forces that relegate the students to a peripheral state of existence that prevents them from fully engaging in the practice to their fullest potential as a student and human being. Marginalization reflects a symbolic and physical particular life situation on the periphery.

2. Throughout the book, I will use the terms *Mexican American, Mexican-descent, Latina/o, Chicana/o,* and *Hispanic* interchangeably, but with all terms meant to describe the ethnicity of the students as being of Mexican origin. Although I note in Chapter 2 that each student self-labeled his or her ethnicity, I still vary the use of the terms above to discuss the student at that point in the book and beyond.

3. All names of students and participants in this study, including the college, are pseudonyms.

# 2

## *Coming from the Margins of School and Life*

### The Students

THE CAMP STUDENT EXPERIENCE, like any student experience, begins with a history. Here we begin with a moving snapshot of who the students were, what they experienced, and how they wrestled with present emotions from the weight of their history as they entered their first year of college. They came with identities formed by disappointment, struggle, and questions about where they came from, where they were going, and who they were becoming as they engaged in the movement toward learning to be a successful student.

As students in this study begin college through CAMP, they are at an intersection of their present identity and the beginning of their movement from a peripheral existence. It is the beginning of new empowered choices they are making. They have chosen to name their realities. They have chosen to react to and reflect on how those present realities have impacted and will continue to impact their lives. This is immediately apparent because of their mere presence in CAMP, and in college. The students have chosen to enact their agency and desire by choosing to apply to CAMP. They have chosen to be resilient by enrolling in college. They have chosen to endure the complications inherent in juggling their present lives, responsibilities, and identities coming from another community of practice into the CAMP community of practice. There are elements of their lives that complicate their trajectory. But they know this. And they have chosen to use these elements of complexity while they embrace this new opportunity for practice and learning.

On the other hand, it is clear that not every marginalized student has choice in their present lived realities. The choice the CAMP students have is one of choosing to go to college or not. But too many marginalized cannot even arrive at a place where they have the ability to choose between a college scholarship or no college scholarship. Often, the choice that many marginalized students make is choosing between the lesser of two evils. And, as such, individuals, ethnicities, races, communities, and cultures are blamed for their present condition, when we know, for example, that no one chooses to be in poverty (Valencia, 1997, 2002).

I think of my first-generation Mexican American mother who married very young, at the age of 15. She dropped out of school in the tenth grade. She then had me at the age of 17. What were *her* choices?

She lived in poverty, her mother constantly absent, her undocumented father working or looking for work, and gone for days at a time. Her siblings took care of her, and she took care of them. Meat like bologna was a luxury. The family looked forward to the summer migrant programs, where they got free meals, candy, and arts and crafts. My father, fresh from a tour of duty in Vietnam, dazzled my mother at a dance, and they married soon thereafter. My very young mother arrived at a crossroads, a choice, and it was an easy one for her to make at the time. That was her choice, a different choice from what the CAMP students have. It is a very different choice from what the privileged have. But my mother still would be labeled, stigmatized, and herded into the dropout-teen-mom, apathetic-toward-education group. What choice did she have?

The CAMP students have arrived at this place in their life trajectory of their own volition. Because they have taken the initiative to apply for the CAMP scholarship, seek out postsecondary education, and enter college, their identities seem grounded in some semblance of hope and a need for movement from their peripheral space. They have chosen to act on this hope. Introducing one student at a time—Laura, Cristina, Luz, Maria, and Ruben—this chapter looks at what each recalls from past schooling experiences, relationships, and formative interactions with others that shaped their present identities as students; the realities of where they stand academically based on the test scores used in many colleges to determine the level of course work they should take; and understanding the movement and tensions in coming from one or many communities of practice into the new CAMP community of practice. This chapter reveals how each student exhibited a different degree of marginalization, some more than others, coming into their first year of college.

## Laura: "He thought there was something wrong with me"

The letter revealed a lot about her.

> Dear Little Laura,
> Be happy. Believe in yourself when others don't believe in you. Always be strong, because there will be people that will try to hurt your feelings for no reason. Don't believe anyone when they tell you that you won't make it just because your [sic] shy. Don't be afraid to say what you really feel. Avoid fake friends, because they don't care about you. Always be a good person and don't let anyone change you.
> Your Future Self,
> Laura

Laura wrote this letter for a career planning assignment in the Computer Applications and Career Planning learning community class. The assignment was to write a letter to your "young self" that reflects on the past to give advice for the future. Although not containing a lot of explicit information, the letter told a great deal about her past, and the nature of her relationships with others. The letter provided a look at how she saw herself as a person, as a student. She saw herself as someone who had been relegated to the edges of social networks in school for a long time because of what she felt was a result of her extreme shyness, reserved nature, and lack of self-confidence. She struggled with joy in her life, as the first directive of her letter

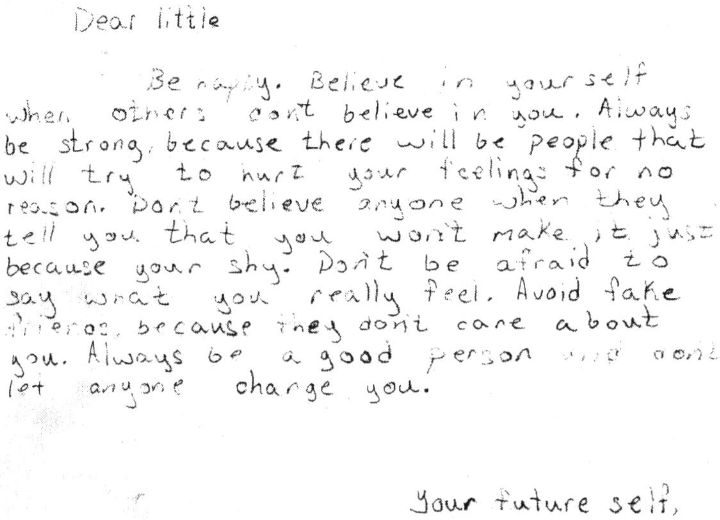

Dear little

Be happy. Believe in yourself when others don't believe in you. Always be strong, because there will be people that will try to hurt your feelings for no reason. Don't believe anyone when they tell you that you won't make it just because your shy. Don't be afraid to say what you really feel. Avoid fake friends, because they don't care about you. Always be a good person and don't let anyone change you.

Your future self,

**Figure 2.1** Laura's letter to self.

indicates—"Be happy." This letter to young Laura reflects a history of experience with others who had little faith in her abilities. It was an expression of her desire to provide herself with self-confidence and agency, even in the face of lack of support or encouragement from others. The issue of "being shy" reflects an expression of her identity that others did not understand and used as a reason for her inability to make it in the world. This took a toll on her self-confidence as a person, and ultimately as a student. She dropped out of high school in the ninth grade. Others had also wanted to "change" her, but, as her letter shows, she was not willing to conform, and simply wanted to "be a good person."

Laura was born in Denver, Colorado, and labeled herself Hispanic. Her mother was born in Texas and her father in Colorado. She spoke only English and was extremely shy and quiet. Throughout my interviews with her, she almost always mentioned something about her shyness. Because of this persona, she did not feel like she could handle the social and academic pressures that went along with being in high school. She said that she "couldn't handle it. Lots of personal things going on. I just really didn't like it." Going into high school, she admitted not having enough self-confidence to go on with her schooling, which ultimately affected both how teachers interacted with her and her academic performance. Her self-confidence and ability to interact and communicate with others was a concern for her going into college and the CAMP program.

Laura qualified for the CAMP program by having participated through the High School Equivalency Program (HEP) and its local partnership with CAMP. Also, her mother was doing what qualified as agricultural work in a greenhouse. Her father worked as a janitor and construction worker. She lived at home with her parents and commuted twenty minutes to school from a nearby town. Her mother finished high school, but her father left school when he was in the eleventh grade. She had a younger brother and sister. Being the first in her family to attend any kind of postsecondary education, Laura was twenty years old when she began college through the CAMP program. She received her GED through the High School Equivalency program before participating in CAMP. It had been five years since she was in a formal school setting, having dropped out of high school when she was fifteen. Her desire was to work with animals as a dog trainer or to be a veterinary technician.

Looking back on when she was in high school, Laura told me that she could not really get close with anyone, especially her teachers. Dropping out of school in the ninth grade contributed to this a great deal. She admitted, "I didn't really have any relationships with the teachers . . . because I left so soon." Laura's lack of relationships with others inside and outside of school perhaps was due to her quiet and shy demeanor. But maybe it was something else. She suggested that her teachers viewed her shyness and lack of participation as more than just a personality trait. She talked about how some saw her as deficient because of her extreme shyness, not really understanding why she would be seen in this way by her teachers. Laura simply was a quiet girl. She just wanted to be in class and do her work. Laura recalls, "I had an English teacher who had us talk about our feelings. I was so quiet and he thought there was something wrong with me. He said I have to go do this 'thing' and I said 'Why? I'm going to miss more class, get more behind.'" The "thing" to which Laura referred was seeing someone, perhaps a counselor or specialist, about her being so quiet in class. I suspect it was a type of behavioral evaluation. Laura did not specify, and she could not recall. In any case, as a result, Laura often felt like she was overlooked by her teachers. In this particular instance, she felt relegated to the outside of the classroom community. She just wanted to keep up with her academic work because she had been falling behind in it, and her teachers could not understand her quiet demeanor. They did not know what to do with someone like Laura. So they defaulted to having others in the school try to figure her out.

Laura had neither the self-confidence nor the skills to successfully engage in and complete her academic work in high school, and the lack of positive attention from her teachers may have contributed to that. Laura "used to miss a lot of days" of school because, she admitted, "it had a lot to do with me not wanting to be there." Because she "couldn't keep up," she was always falling further behind in her work; she mentioned that she was afraid to seek the help she needed, because she thought it would make her appear even more incapable or deficient to her teachers. Laura believed that she "wasn't pushed by parents or teachers or anyone." She felt that the people she looked up to were essentially giving up on her, not encouraging her in her academic efforts, which made her not care about school either. She was conflicted about her role and efforts in her education and those roles that adult figures played in her schooling. It was a cycle that eventually led to her leaving school. Laura partially blames herself for leaving high school by suggesting that "maybe I was lazy." But she also felt that she could have benefited from being in an environment at home or school that created opportunities for her to engage in school more effectively by being "pushed" more by others. Laura's belief that others did not care about her schooling had a great impact on her valuing and desiring to continue with her schooling.

Laura stated that soon after dropping out (or being pushed out) of high school and having low-paying jobs with little possibility for career advancement, "I wanted to make a change in my life, instead of just staying home or with a job I didn't like. I wanted a career." After beginning school through CAMP, she realized that her attitude toward work, school, and her future changed very quickly: "Now, a lot of my thinking has changed toward school. I want to do it. I want to work hard to have a good career and support my family in the future."

Laura believed that she "blew" her chance for college when she dropped out of high school. Before starting college and the CAMP program, she was scared: "I thought it was gonna be hard, but I mean not something I couldn't handle but . . . I thought, I guess before, I thought it was far from my reach, like, I couldn't, you know, possibly be here." She admitted she was afraid because of her low self-confidence in doing schoolwork. She did not feel that she was adequately prepared to do the work required for college, stating that it was "maybe low self-esteem or because I was out of school for so long. I didn't think that, I guess, I had the brain power to do it." Going into college and the CAMP program, Laura still doubted her motivation and ability to push herself beyond what she was accustomed to in her educational efforts. There was a lingering fear that others would not be there to "push" her, so she would have to create this sense of agency on her own. She was not sure she could do it, though.

Like all students who entered Next Step Community College, Laura was required to take the computer-based Accuplacer test to determine in what courses she would be placed. The Accuplacer tests a student's academic skills in math, English, and reading. The scores are used to inform academic advisers or counselors about which courses, developmental or college-level, the students should take. For example, students had to score at least a 70 on the Reading Comprehension test in order to be placed in a beginning, college-level English course (numbered 100 or above at NSCC). Any courses at or below ENG 090 were developmental and not for transferable college credit. Some of the students in the CAMP program scored high enough to place into college-level courses. Others were not able to score a 70 and thus were placed in a developmental course, for which they did not receive college-level course credit. Students also had to score a minimum of 50 on their Elementary Algebra Accuplacer test in order to be placed in a college-level math course.

Although Laura scored high enough in the English portion of her Accuplacer test, it was decided that she be placed in a developmental English course, ENG 090–Basic Composition. Because her Accuplacer Elementary Algebra math score was so low, she was placed in a developmental course, MAT 030–Fundamentals of Mathematics. This was a common issue among many of the CAMP

TABLE 2.1. Laura's Accuplacer Scores

| Accuplacer Test | Score |
|---|---|
| Reading comprehension | 76 |
| Sentence skills | 90 |
| Elementary algebra | 22 |
| Arithmetic | 33 |

students—academic underpreparation. This reflects the trend that many high school students in general are not ready for college coursework and that there is a disconnect in how they are prepared academically between high school and college (Greene and Forster, 2003; Kirst and Venezia, 2001; McCarthy and Kuh, 2006). None of the CAMP participants were on a college track in high school that would have adequately prepared them for college. However, Luz did take Spanish AP courses. Very low math scores were common among all five students discussed here, while the Reading and Sentence scores varied.

## Concluding Thoughts on Laura's History

Laura was extremely shy and introverted, which was a personality trait misunderstood by her peers, teachers, and family. She felt that little was expected of her school performance, because she felt that no one really "pushed" her to excel academically, which resulted in her disconnect from school—academically and socially. Her educational marginalization occurred early in high school. Part of this was a result of a stigma attached to the "difference" of Laura's complex personality that was unlike those of other students and people in the mainstream, perpetuating a cycle of misunderstanding. Teachers dealt with her "difference" from other students by assuming she had a deficiency (personal and/or academic) and simply relegating her to the margins of schooling experience. Although Laura said that she did make a concerted effort to resist the temptation to leave school, her parents did not confront her on the issue of school or "push" her in her academic and social efforts in high school. This allowed her to leave school without attempting to reconcile these issues.

Her social and educational marginalization affected her self-confidence as a student, planting doubts about the possibilities of succeeding in college. She did not have experience in the practice of being a successful student in her adolescent years, creating a gap in her schooling and ultimately a lack of preparation for college-level coursework, especially in writing and math. Because the CAMP scholarship did provide an opportunity for Laura to engage in the practice of being a successful student, this was an opportunity to test herself and be surrounded by others who provided support in her endeavors.

## Cristina: "We were just ordinary kids that wanted to go to college"

Cristina was just two months from turning 19 when she began college. She was quiet in class but opened up to people and instructors when it was necessary (e.g., asking about schoolwork, scholarships, CAMP requirements). She was very ambitious in her schoolwork. That is, she wanted to do well academically and make good grades, often staying after class to clarify assignments with instructors or seeking additional help from the CAMP coordinator. But with English as her second language, Cristina sometimes doubted her abilities; she felt her English was not strong enough to be the student she really wanted to be. Even though she was single and had no children, Cristina had many financial and other responsibilities at home, because her father was no longer around, and she had to help her mother and her sisters.

Cristina was born in the United States and grew up in a Spanish-speaking household. Her parents were born in rural Mexico. Both parents finished school at the sixth grade and then found jobs to support the family. During the CAMP program, she lived at home, only five minutes away from campus. Cristina's father was not present at the time of this study; her parents had divorced and he had moved back to Mexico, but he would come back from time to time. There were tensions and conflict with her father. Part of this tension appeared to be rooted in a clashing of identities and changing perceptions of roles within their household. Perhaps his leaving was a result of not being able to deal with his diminishing patriarchal power and the need to share that power with the women of the family (Hondagneu-Sotelo, 1992). Cristina, her older sister, and mother all had to contribute to the family finances. She worked to help pay certain bills, such as electricity and phone, which supplemented the overall family income. Her mother worked on a hen farm, where she handled and packed eggs. But the work and educational discourse was changing in her family, an allusion to who and what Cristina might eventually become. She wanted to go to college. She wanted to get a four-year degree that would allow her to work with people and children, but for a long time this goal seemed elusive.

Cristina did well in school because of her natural desire to do well in everything she did. However, at some point in her life and schooling, she was socialized to believe that college would not be an option for her, a sentiment common to many Latinas, especially those who are children of immigrants (Zell, 2010). Cristina recalls:

> When I was growing up, I wanted to do different stuff. I really wanted to go to college, but deep down inside I knew that college wasn't an option. As a little girl, graduating [from high school] would be my biggest goal; that would be the best thing I could do for myself. College was not even in my thoughts. I went to the same school, I started in preschool there, and I graduated there. My mom doesn't speak English, and the teachers would be, like, okay, go home and do your homework with your parents. Next day, I would say, yeah, I did my homework with my mom, and things like that. Kids have to lie just to fit in, and that used to always happen to me. They would say, get involved with your parents, sit down and do your homework, and my mom was always busy. My mom really cared about us and reminded us to do our homework, but she'd get home really late and be trying to cook and clean and do laundry. Plus, she didn't know how to speak English, so she couldn't help me. My mom was really supportive about going to school. My dad was just there, but . . . I think I did pretty good growing up and in middle school. I had pretty good grades, I was a good student.

Cristina accepted her mother for who she was. She understood the sacrifices she had to make to support the family and Cristina's educational endeavors. Her mother's support for her education refutes the general belief that parents of Mexican descent do not support their children in school or do not believe that education is important (Valencia and Black, 2002). The way(s) that Cristina's mother supported her also reflect how Mexican-descent parents support their children's educational endeavors in different ways (Auerbach, 2006; Ceja, 2004). Cristina loved school, but for what seemed to be a lack of interest or ability to tap into her potential in school, her high school experience did not provide a schooling experience and curriculum plan that would nurture her desire to excel. Her school also did not understand that for bilingual students like Cristina whose mother could not speak English, getting help with homework in English was not possible.

Cristina's attitude toward high school was deterministic. High school was an experience that she simply wanted to finish because, she said, "I wouldn't get a scholarship, so I wasn't coming to college. I just wanted to graduate and it didn't matter." Cristina did not perceive herself as a possible college student when in high school. She was never informed about the importance of the need for preparation for postsecondary education. She believed that college would be inaccessible, because she thought that her high school did not foster a schooling experience that encouraged students like her to pursue higher-level and more challenging courses that provided preparation for college. In looking back on her high school experience, she felt that she could have done more to be better prepared for college. Cristina wished she would have been more involved, but having to work many hours after school to help with family finances did not allow it. What were her choices? It was apparent that in her high school experience she was "schooled" and socialized to believe that college would not be an option.

Cristina put a great deal of the responsibility of creating possibilities and opportunities for schooling experiences and learning on herself. Although, in reflecting on the practices of her high school in challenging students like her and providing opportunities to prepare for college, she began to talk about what they "should have done." She thus expressed a conflicted and ambiguous understanding of student-versus-school roles in the education process by again blaming herself for her lack of involvement, while also feeling the school could have done more for her. She felt that someone or something in her high school experience should have actively informed and encouraged students like her to "take more requirements" to better prepare for college, because she "just did the basics and missed out on so much." Taking the college computer placement test and having to take "developmental courses" that were not for college credit made her feel underprepared and uncomfortable. But this is a common sentiment among students who test into remedial courses when entering college (Bettinger and Long, 2009). Contradictorally, she suggested, "I know it's my fault, but I know they (her high school) could have done something, and try to get you more involved, and make you understand." Cristina's sentiments and experience reflect what Venezia and Kirst (2005) critique in the K–12 system and its inability to adequately inform and prepare students, in particular first-generation students like Cristina, for college culture, expectations, and coursework. Cristina knew that her life situation and obligations during high school prevented her from being more involved but felt that the school also had some responsibility in providing more options and possibilities for preparing for college in their curriculum.

Cristina did not feel academically prepared to go to college, which contributed to some apprehension. During high school, she took the lowest level of courses she needed to graduate, what she called the "basic classes." As mentioned earlier, Cristina did not feel that her high school adequately prepared her for the rigors of college, which was reflected in her being tracked in the basic courses she described. For many Latinas like Cristina, this ability tracking for low-income English learners is often the result of lack of resources and preparation to even be ready to take courses that would prepare them for college (Faltis and Arias, 1993; Gándara and Contreras, 2009; González, Stoner, and Jovel, 2003). Cristina also was not comfortable with her level of English, thinking that she would not know enough to do college-level work. This phenomenon is very common with English learners, who often acquire social language more easily and faster than the more complex academic language needed to do well in school (Cummins, 2000). She suggested that she knew "a little bit of English and a little bit of Spanish," which may reflect not only the idea that she knows just enough of both languages to simply get by on both social and academic levels, but also the low level of confidence in her academic abilities in school.

As Cristina mentioned, she took courses that did not prepare her for college-level coursework. She was tracked into a basic curriculum that provided the minimum of core content courses and electives to graduate. In high school, she took Integrated Algebra and Integrated Geometry as her highest math courses, while taking Short Fiction and Creative Writing for her most advanced English courses. Cristina's Accuplacer scores placed her in ENG 060–Writing Fundamentals, and in MAT 060–Pre-Algebra. She admitted that perhaps these courses were what she needed, because she knew she would not do well in higher-level courses at the time. She did not feel ready. The English course was especially critical in building up her English skills and confidence in writing.

For Cristina, going to college meant something beyond herself. She was motivated by both personal and community- and family-oriented reasons. She said, "I've always wanted to come to college. One of my obstacles was money for college. I want to change my generation, because I'm like the first person to go to college in my family." Cristina cried when she talked about how much her mother worked and how she appreciated her. She was very close to her mother. Cristina recognized how hard her mother's life was—from dealing with the violence of an abusive husband, to working constantly for little money. Helping her mother was a driving force behind her going to college:

> But, I mean, nobody knows what you live through, my mom and my dad lived together for a very long time, and my dad was an asshole. He was bad to my mom, and my mom paid

TABLE 2.2. Cristina's Accuplacer Scores

| Accuplacer Test | Score |
| --- | --- |
| Reading comprehension | 66 |
| Sentence skills | 71 |
| Elementary algebra | 32 |
| Arithmetic | 34 |

everything. My dad would make really good money and then spend it. And now that we're by ourselves, life is calm, life is really calm, I mean, you don't have a guy macho-drinking and all this. But if it's hard, it's hard [begins to cry] because I see my mom working so hard, and she wakes up at three in the morning just to make us something to eat. She still gets home and tries to clean the house and make food. That's why I just want to work and help her out, and I don't know if my goal right now is to go to college. I want to do both, I want to work and help her, but at the same time I just want to keep on going to school.

One of Cristina's motivations for school was financial and material. But she was conflicted because she also wanted so badly to just work and help her mother financially, a sentiment common for many Latinas in their transition to college (Sy, 2006). She wanted something better for her mother. She didn't like the house her mother was living in and said, "I want to get her out of there. I don't plan to get married for a long time. My goal right now is just to go to college and to have a job. And to graduate with a little major, and buy my mom a little house, be with her." But to accomplish this, she knew she had to continue with college, even if just working part-time while doing so. For Cristina, going to college provided a sense of purpose beyond herself. This reflects what Zell (2010) found in her examination of Latinas' experiences in a community college and issues of persistence and completion. Latina students like Cristina felt that achieving a college education would give them the opportunity to give back to family and community. A college education is almost a sense of obligation to those who sacrificed for them. Cristina wanted to give something back to her mother by completing college.

Cristina was also motivated by a desire to prove her capabilities and potential success to her father. When asked what role her estranged father had in her life and educational pursuits, she admitted that his negativity created positive motivation.

My dad never believed in me. I was the first one born here. My older sister was born in Mexico. He used to tell me, just because you're Chicana, you think you're all this and that, and I think that kind of . . . I told my mom today, I want to go back to Mexico and prove my dad wrong someday. I want to go and be a successful woman and go see him, because he used to always tell me that I was not going to be anything and I thought I was this and that because I was born here, and I want to prove him wrong. So that is something that is in the back of my mind. I have to do it, because he'd always not believe in me.

Cristina's estranged relationship with her father is rooted in a tension of natal histories. Her father, born in and again living in Mexico after leaving the family, resented her for being born in the United States, which in turn resulted in her resentment of his bitterness and lack of faith in who she was. One result of this tension was/ is a power struggle between Cristina and her father. He may have felt threatened by her Chicana identity, one that represents not only being born in the United States but all the privileges that come with it. But the "Chicana" label was assigned to Cristina by her father. According to Matute-Bianchi (2008) and her categorization of students of Mexican descent, Cristina would actually be considered Mexican-oriented, someone who maintains a strong Mexican identity, using English and Spanish interchangeably but has lived most of her life in the United States. Cristina's father used this label of "Chicana" to demean her, and perhaps for her to question her loyalty to her ethnic identity. It did not reflect her academic performance in school. The Chicanos in Matute-Bianchi's study were students who were not academically motivated, contrary to the identity and efforts of Cristina, who wanted to do well in school and desired success. But Cristina interpreted her father's name-calling, actions, and attitudes toward her partly as a lack of faith in her ability to do well in school and life; "he never believed" in her. Cristina is using both anger and desire to fuel her current trajectory in learning to be a successful student, feelings intensified by a clash of Mexican and Chicano histories, geographies, and identities.

When asked how she felt about beginning college, Cristina admitted she was not comfortable with the idea: "I was nervous. I didn't feel I would come to college. I didn't apply for any scholarships in high school, I felt like I was just going to graduate and start work, because I didn't have any opportunities to start. I can't afford college."

She acknowledged that it was hard for her to believe that the CAMP program gave her and the other CAMP students the attention they were receiving. She believed such attention was reserved for privileged and academically superior students, stating, "We were just all ordinary students . . . we're not straight-A students . . . because usually students that have the best grades in high school, As and 4.0s, get all the scholarships, and we were just ordinary kids that wanted to go to college. They were offering us everything. That was shocking, because I was just an ordinary girl graduating from high school, and I just got this one year of college scholarship."

## Concluding Thoughts on Cristina's History

Cristina felt she was misguided in her high school experience. Although she felt she carried some responsibility for her lack of participation in classes that would better prepare her for college-level work, she knew that her high school could have done more to guide her in that pursuit. She was motivated, determined, and desired success, but was led to believe that students like herself could not or would not go to college. This was reflected in her high school's inability to provide other curriculum opportunities for her so that she could be better prepared for college coursework. Similarly, Zell (2010) also found in her study that Latina community college students had to overcome a negative self-perception that was socially constructed in their precollege schooling experience. The Latinas she interviewed expressed that they left high school believing that college was not for them, or that they were not academically prepared for college, so why bother? Cristina felt that the teachers and/or counselors failed to recognize her potential to take more challenging courses and bring to the surface her desire to attend college. The school's recruiting and information sessions for Chicana/o students like Cristina were superficial and scant at best. They seemed to lack a component of motivational dynamics that would convince Chicana/o students to pursue higher education in her high school.

Cristina was also burdened with the responsibility of contributing to the family finances, which took a toll on her academic performance and her desire to participate more in school activities. Because she felt that there was no possibility of attending college, mainly for financial reasons, she attended and finished high school for the sake of getting it done. She "just wanted to graduate and it didn't matter." She planned on continuing to work at low-paying jobs to continue to help her family financially.

In her early experiences of college through CAMP, Cristina was not sure she would be adequately prepared for college-level course-work because of the lack of preparation and rigor in her high school experience. Because Cristina went through high school believing that college would never be an option, her identity as a potential college student was marginal upon entering the college and CAMP community of practice. Cristina's student identity at that point in her schooling reflected the entrenched internalization of a deficit per-spective of academic abilities, the idea that she was incapable of the rigors of college-level work because of who she was or what she was tracked into in school (Valencia, 2002; Valenzuela, 1999). Cristina lacked confidence in many of her academic abilities, especially in the English language. As a student, she was unsure that someone like her even belonged in college, because she thought college and scholar-ships were for students who "had the best grades" and were not for "ordinary students."

## Luz: "Please . . . don't fall in love so easily"

Luz was a quiet and serious girl, who almost always kept to herself in and outside of class. Only when she was in situations where she had to interact with others throughout the program did she work with, talk to, and socialize with the students and CAMP staff. She was quiet because she spoke only when she had something to say. Her seriousness stemmed from her attitude toward life and school. She knew she had to work hard and be dedicated to get anywhere in life. For most of her young life, she had been working either in the home helping with chores or in the fields during the summers with her family.

Luz was 18 years old at the time of this study. She was single, born in Denver, Colorado, and identified as Hispanic. She spoke both Spanish and English well. Her parents were born in San Luis

Potosí, Mexico, and worked in agriculture for most of their lives in the United States. Her father went to school until the third grade, while her mother went until the second grade. She lived with her parents and had a part-time job. They were very supportive of her schooling efforts.

She had six sisters, all older, who graduated from high school as well. Two took one or two classes at the local college, but Luz was the first to attend full-time and will be the first to complete a degree. All her sisters married and had children young, which she often discussed. In fact, she was often fearful of falling into the same situation as her sisters, which she believed would prevent her from achieving her educational and professional goals. After seeing her sisters struggle as young mothers, she knew she did not want to follow on that same path. She wanted to be a registered nurse and aspired to get her master's degree in nursing. In high school, she took AP classes in Spanish language and literature, classes that college-bound students typically take. Her Spanish teacher, Ms. Rivas, and her counselor, Mr. Fernandez, often encouraged her to pursue college. But Luz still grappled with the vision of college as a possibility. It was not clear to her that she could be a successful college student.

Even though Luz came from a migrant and agricultural working family, she did not admit to experiencing the type of educational marginalization that so many migrant students do in the United States, dealing with issues of incompatibility between her and her schooling (Cárdenas, 1995). If she missed school, she was usually able to catch up very quickly. There were times, however, when she wasn't able to keep up with her schoolwork, which affected her grades. She and her family often did migrant work during the summer months through September or October, in Colorado. Her parents sought different, temporary jobs throughout the remainder of the year, exhibiting habits of settled migrancy, where they remained close to home and traveled little when working during the harvesting seasons and working in the fields.

Luz, like her sisters, was a key contributing member of the family operation. Her bilingual skills helped her parents conduct important tasks, a generational phenomenon common to bilingual children of immigrants or migrants (Morales and Hanson, 2005; Tse, 1995).

In elementary school, I already understood a lot of English. I spoke a lot of English in elementary school because I had to, so I picked it up quickly. I spoke Spanish at home. Now I speak all Spanish at home. My parents don't speak English. They do, but only when they need to, at work sometimes, or when they go to the doctor. They know what they need to say or use in English. But usually they'll take me along with them because they're not so sure. So I have to go with them, and it still happens a lot.

Luz also contributed physical labor for additional family income. But she was aware of the contrasts in the types of work required for school versus that of migrant agricultural work. "When I used to work in the fields, I used to prefer going to school. I'd rather be in school listening to a teacher, even though it was a pain in the butt. I'd prefer that, because it was so hot and tiring. We had to get things done. We had to work fast. If you stayed behind, then no money. You just had to go fast, fast."

Luz was accustomed to hard work, as it also showed in her efforts in school. She graduated in the top 16 percent of her class with a 3.2 GPA. For much of her school life, Luz was unsure of the purpose of college. For most of her high school life, she was intent on just finishing high school, starting a family, and getting a job. But her Spanish teacher in high school, Ms. Rivas, encouraged her, even "pushed" her, to look at college as a possibility and even an inevitability. Ms. Rivas saw great potential in her student. Luz explains: "Now I see that if people tell me to do something, I know I can, because she [Ms. Rivas] would push me towards it. If I was able to do that, why can't I do anything else I want?" Luz acknowledged that she never would have applied for the CAMP scholarship or even considered going to college if it weren't for her Spanish teacher. It was mostly individual teachers in high school that encouraged and informed her about the opportunities college had to offer. Similar to Cristina's experience, the school as an institution had little to do with creating a school climate and culture that promoted and pushed college on their students, much less students like Luz. Nonetheless, Luz said that the individual attention made her feel special, and stated that in her high school many of the teachers would encourage students who saw potential in them to succeed in college.

As to coursework and academic experiences in high school, she talked about having taken particular classes that she felt were affecting what she was doing in college. Luz wished she had never been in ESL and that she had taken higher-level math in high school. She soon realized that some of the earlier courses she took in her first quarter at Next Step Community College through CAMP were not college-level and that she would not receive college credit.

Luz's marginalization was complex. Academically, she did well. She had high personal, academic, and professional aspirations. But she often felt torn between her personal ambitions and the fear that romance, love, and a committed relationship with a man would impede her plans. Much of this fear was fueled by the expectations of young women from her distant family in Mexico to marry and have children young. Although her parents supported her schooling efforts, the lack of support from geographically distant relatives managed to have an effect on her self-perception and ambitions. These discourses weighed heavily on Luz, often distracting her and keeping her from being an active participant in the CAMP community of practice.

The influence of relatives in Mexico and in the United States was a constant presence in her life. The family was very close, so they would often be at her home, or others in Mexico would call. Visits to Mexico would consist of many conversations between her father and her aunts and uncles about Luz and her future. They would talk to her father about Luz attending college, but they were not very supportive. Luz expressed

> My relatives, my cousins, my aunts . . . they would all say, you're just wasting your time, you're going to get married, that's all you're studying for. That's in a way why, when I was in high school, I questioned why I would go to college. My aunts and uncles tried to discourage me from college. They told me that education was a waste of time; that I should just get married. They said it would be a waste of my parents' money.

Despite the influence of relatives, Luz's parents still supported her. Going back to her high school days, the influence of this discourse from distant family had a long history. But it still triggered fears of what she viewed as a potential obstacle that romance and commitment

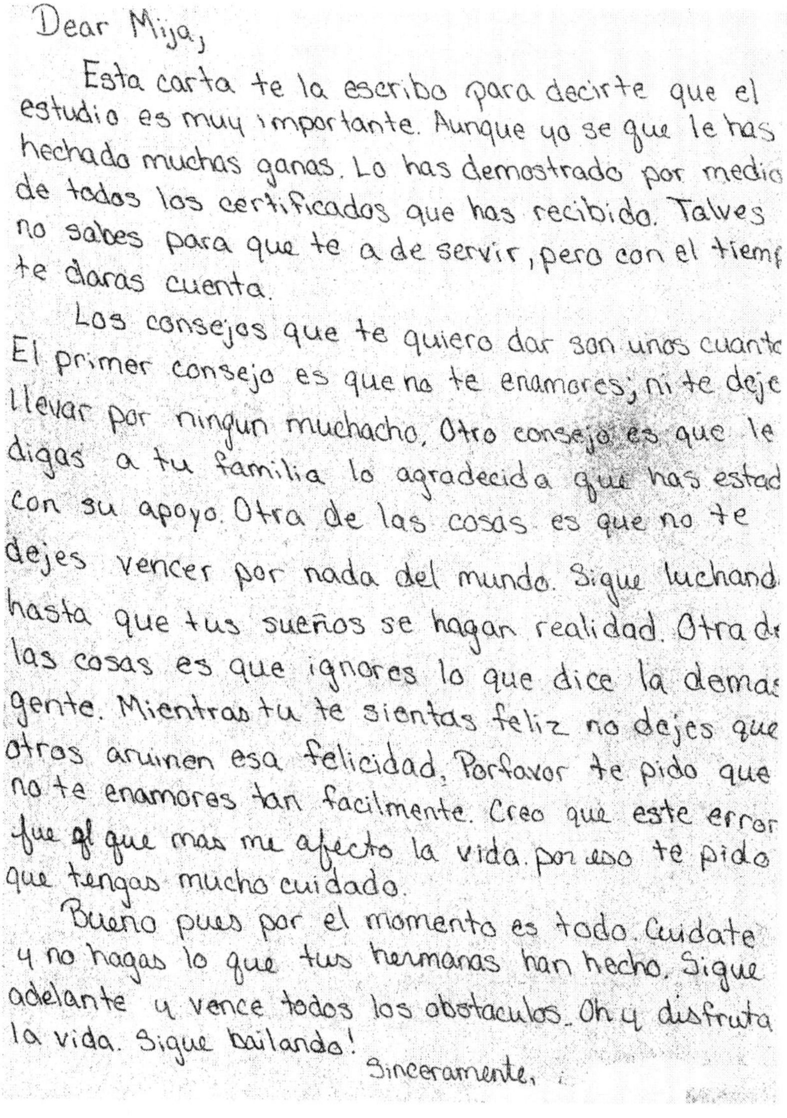

Dear Mija,

Esta carta te la escribo para decirte que el estudio es muy importante. Aunque yo se que le has hechado muchas ganas. Lo has demostrado por medio de todos los certificados que has recibido. Talves no sabes para que te a de servir, pero con el tiemp te daras cuenta.

Los consejos que te quiero dar son unos cuant El primer consejo es que no te enamores; ni te deje llevar por ningun muchacho. Otro consejo es que le digas a tu familia lo agradecida que has estad con su apoyo. Otra de las cosas es que no te dejes vencer por nada del mundo. Sigue luchand hasta que tus sueños se hagan realidad. Otra d las cosas es que ignores lo que dice la demas gente. Mientras tu te sientas feliz no dejes que otros aruinen esa felicidad. Porfavor te pido que no te enamores tan facilmente. Creo que este error fue el que mas me afecto la vida. por eso te pido que tengas mucho cuidado.

Bueno pues por el momento es todo. Cuidate y no hagas lo que tus hermanas han hecho. Sigue adelante y vence todos los obstaculos. Oh y disfruta la vida. Sigue bailando!

Sinceramente,

**Figure 2.2**  Luz's letter to self.

could be in her educational endeavors. She did not think that school and having a relationship could be done simultaneously.

Below is the letter (translated to English) that Luz wrote to her "young self" in the Career Planning course.

> Dear Little Luz,
>
> This letter is to tell you that education is very important. I know that you have put forth a lot of effort in school, which is shown through all the awards and certificates you have won. You might not know what purpose they will serve, but with time you will discover why.
>
> I want to give you some advice. The first thing is don't fall in love and let a guy take you away from what you are doing now. And tell your family how thankful you are to them for their support. Don't let anything overcome you. Keep on fighting until your dreams become a reality. Ignore what others have to say about you and don't let them get in the way of your happiness. Please, I'm telling you, don't fall in love so easily. I think the chance of making this mistake bothers me the most. Just be careful.
>
> That's all for now. Be careful and don't do what your sisters have done. Keep going and overcome all those obstacles. And another thing—enjoy life and keep dancing!
>
> Sincerely,
>
> Luz

Luz's biggest fears were rooted in the possibility of romance, a relationship, and domesticity getting in the way of accomplishing her goals. These fears motivated her but also planted doubts as to whether she was doing the right thing by not marrying and having children at an early age like her sisters.

Her boyfriend wanted a serious relationship, while she did not. At least not at the time. She was too afraid of where it would lead. Below is a vignette from field notes on an interaction with Luz, which illustrates the lingering pressures of romance on her.

> I see Luz at a table in the student lounge and CAMP office. Another CAMP student is sitting at one round table, while Luz is

at my table, and Israel [CAMP counselor] is sitting on the edge
of a sofa next to Luz. We ask Luz how she is doing because we
hadn't seen her for awhile. She tells us that she's having a hard
time focusing on her studies right now because she is getting
"pressure" from her boyfriend, who is not being very supportive of her education, while her parents are telling her to ignore
her boyfriend, whom she loves very much, and to concentrate
on her education. Education has always been important to Luz.
She wants to become a nurse and is doing everything she possibly can to do so. She tells us that the pressure is getting to her.
Israel gives her some advice, as do I, about not being around
negative people and people who are not going to support her,
that she should stay away from them. Israel offers to talk to
her boyfriend if she'd like. She says she'll think about it and
then Israel has to leave to work with another student. The other
CAMP student leaves too. I continue to talk to Luz about how
she should just talk to her boyfriend about her feelings and tell
him that if he really loves her, that he wouldn't be the way he
is being and that he should just support her. She just nods her
head, begins to cry, and says, "it's just hard." I give her some
Kleenex and again she says "it's just hard."

Even with support from family and friends, Luz still was conflicted.
Luz did not always think that she was college material, even
though she made good grades and was always complimented by her
teachers on her academic abilities. In middle school she would get
As and Bs; her high school years were a bit more erratic, but she
still graduated with a GPA of 3.2 at the rank of 24 out of a class of
146 students. She mentioned how her parents would move back and
forth from the United States to Mexico, which sometimes took a toll
on her academic performance and her ability to see herself as someone who was equipped to continue her education after high school.
When asked if she thought she was college material before starting
the program, she replied, "No. I didn't think so. I thought it was
only for smart people. I considered it hard, too, college being very
hard." She did confess that, "To me, when they said, do you want to
go to college, for me college was just for rich people. Just for people

who had money, maybe geeks too. People who liked school, I guess, doing homework. That's the way I saw college before."

When she first applied for the CAMP scholarship, she was very apathetic about the entire process, even pessimistic about the notion of winning an academic scholarship to attend college. She said that "in a way, I really didn't care . . . because I didn't think I would go to college. I applied...but then after the scholarship awards in high school and Angie [NSCC/CAMP recruiter] announced my name, I was stunned, and I got also a prize. I was surprised because I had doubted I would get it." She admitted that soon thereafter she discovered the costs of attending college and was grateful for the CAMP scholarship.

A successful student, to Luz, was someone who got good grades, understood the material being taught, and remembered what they learned. She was very pragmatic about the entire schooling process and what steps to take to accomplish her goals. For Luz, college was "just succeeding in higher education. You don't struggle as when you graduate from high school and then work at a company and are not being paid very well. I guess college is something for me where I can get paid more than that. Work in an environment I would like, such as nursing." For Luz, college was equipping herself to get into a profession that she could enjoy and that would provide a good salary.

Luz did feel academically prepared to attend college, even though at one point she had heard "about it being very difficult, or that teachers wouldn't be there to help me, so that's what I was afraid of." She was afraid that she would have no assistance with her academics and her adjustment to college because she did not think she was personally equipped to do so. Those fears subsided, though, when she recalled what she had learned from some of her teachers in high school. She told me that her Spanish teacher in particular pushed her beyond her comfort zone into more challenging academics that helped her see herself as a capable student. She said her teacher "really encouraged me, and she really believed in me. She thought I'd be successful, and she said that it wouldn't be hard."

Luz had to take some developmental courses in the first quarter of college and the program, based on her Accuplacer scores. She often expressed her discomfort with this fact and felt like some of the courses she was taking were a waste of time, because she already wanted to be in a nursing program. But she learned to be patient and was comforted when she realized that these courses were necessary to help her get where she wanted to be in her education. Her first English and math courses were ENG 060, Writing Fundamentals, taken in the first quarter, and MAT 080, Mathematics and Basic Algebra, taken in the second quarter.

## Concluding Thoughts on Luz's History

Luz's marginalization stemmed from competing discourses—her desire to continue her college and career ambitions and the fear of romance and domesticity. Much of this tension was fueled by the words of unsupportive relatives. She internalized this tension, which often pressured and confused her. Luz did not believe that she could do college while being in a serious relationship. She feared that marriage and children would derail her educational and professional pursuits. Luz's fears are not unfounded. They are reminiscent of what Holland and Eisenhart (1990) found in their study of the culture of romance and relationships and its role in the academic and professional pursuits of women in college—"romantic relationships both affected and were affected by their experiences with schoolwork" (p. 213). It was the influence of educators, especially her Spanish teacher, who was Latina, in her high school years that began to contribute to the agency of her strong work ethic and solid academic skills that equipped her with envisioning the possibility of attending college. This placed her on a trajectory toward developing a sense of being and becoming a successful student. But she still had to contend with influential discourses that were pulling her in different directions and making her think twice about who she was, what she was doing, and where she was going.

TABLE 2.3. Luz's Accuplacer Scores

| Accuplacer Test | Score |
| --- | --- |
| Reading comprehension | 55 |
| Sentence skills | 72 |
| Elementary algebra | 40 |
| Arithmetic | 75 |

## Maria: "When I got pregnant,
## I just wanted to stop"

Like Laura, Cristina, and Luz, Maria had a quiet demeanor about her. But she was always willing to talk about life. As a single, 20-year-old mother of two young boys, she had already learned so much. She had to. Coming into CAMP, she was filled with anticipation of a hope that at times was difficult for her to find.

Maria received her GED in 2001, and began 2002–2003 CAMP in the second quarter of the academic year. She was not able to participate in many of the early-year CAMP activities but still benefited from the other financial, academic, and human resources that the program offered. Maria labeled herself as Hispanic. Her mother was born in Florida, and her father in Texas. She was born in Loveland, Colorado, and had worked only odd jobs in the fast-food industry. She was living with her mother and sister, whose combined total annual income was $15,000 at the time.

Maria came from a family with four girls. Her father was always strict and protective of his daughters. Maybe too protective. She described her situation with her family as "hard" and said that she didn't have a good relationship with her father. Life was even more difficult when she got pregnant in the tenth grade and dropped out of school. With tears falling, Maria recalls how emotional the situation was for her when she told her parents, admitting that her father hit her when he found out.

Maria felt like she could have done better in high school if she had received more individual help. She found it helpful when someone explained the work by showing her how to do it. This type of help was not common or available to Maria in high school. She said that "they just wanted you to hand in the work, whether it was right or wrong. If it was wrong, they would try to explain, but it was hard without a tutor." Maria needed one-on-one help with her coursework to explain difficult concepts, but this help was hard to come by for her in high school.

In school, nobody ever encouraged Maria to go to college or take the courses needed to enter college and be prepared. Her mother was the only one who discussed the value of attending college and getting an education. She said that she really was not "pushed" by anyone to excel in school or to investigate what was required to pursue college. She said, "I thought it was hard to get in, but I didn't know about the financial aid, scholarships, anything like that." Maria was not aware of the steps required to gain entry to college and how to pursue financial assistance. But she knew she needed to get a college degree to get a good job.

Maria said her worst time in high school was "when I got pregnant, that was the only time my academics were kind of hard, but I always tried to keep them up. But I never had anything worse than that or anything bad. I struggled, but tried my best." She told me that she didn't remember any positive experiences in high school. It was "just school." Her pregnancy and all that surrounded it in her family constituted a critical time in her life and changed her forever. She said, "When I got pregnant, I just wanted to stop. I didn't want anything. I didn't want to do anything." Because her father was devastated by her pregnancy and angry, it created a deep rift in their relationship. She received no support from her father, but her mother was there to help in various ways.

For Maria, the actual act of being in college was a sign of progression up the social and educational ladder. She suggested that "actually even coming to college is one step, being successful; also when I find out that I'm going to be going to another college, when I'm finished here and ready to go on to a bigger college, I think that that's being successful." Maria admitted no fears about starting college. She was more looking forward to the experience than apprehensive. She said, "No, I wasn't nervous. I was more excited than nervous. I told my mom I couldn't wait until I started school. I wasn't nervous or anything, even if I didn't know anybody. I wasn't scared or anything."

Maria did not feel she was academically prepared to begin college, though, because of a two-year gap between her high school experience and beginning college, the amount of time it took to earn her GED. Her academic skills were not adequate in preparing her for college coursework, especially in English and Math. She also struggled with how to use a computer. She expressed, though, "I'm prepared now to learn everything they're teaching me. I dropped out of high school in 10th grade, 16 years old. I have two kids, three and two. Both boys." She hinted that her leaving high school and having the responsibility of two young boys would be a factor in her schooling.

She knew that it would be a challenge to do school while being a young mother of two. Nonetheless, she had the desire and readiness to pursue her education.

When asked what she liked about being in the CAMP program, she suggested that part of her comfort with it was that it accepted someone like her, a teen mother, who had experienced academic, personal, and financial troubles in the past. She said, "I like the fact that I got accepted. I didn't think I was going to, and I told my mom I was worried because what if financial aid didn't help me? It was a big thing that I was actually accepted in the program."

Maria's Accuplacer scores placed her in ENG 060–Writing Fundamentals and MAT 030–Fundamentals of Mathematics. Maria often struggled with academics and needed individual attention to grasp various concepts. She acknowledged that having that type of support in the CAMP program was helpful in her learning.

The letters that the students wrote to their "young self" also were a form of a more knowledgeable other providing advice, comfort, and encouragement. The letters were a nexus of past, present, and future wisdom. Maria's "letter to self" that she wrote in the Computer/Career Planning learning community course provided insight into some personal struggles that she carried with her into her college experience:

Young Maria ("Skinny Girl"),

Hi Maria! It's me again. I've been here your whole life. I'll always be here for you whenever you need me. But I am telling you right now, there are alot [*sic*] of challenges in life, that we have gone through together. Don't ever let anyone tell you what to do. Just because you have to [*sic*] kids of your own doesn't mean you won't be able to do anything in life. As of

TABLE 2.4. Maria's Accuplacer Scores

| Accuplacer Test | Score |
|---|---|
| Reading comprehension | 56 |
| Sentence skills | 49 |
| Elementary algebra | 31 |
| Arithmetic | 28 |

right now everyone thinks you are doing good so far, so don't
ever let yourself down, because you have a long ways to go. So
take care of yourself and your kids. Take everything day by day.
   Always,
   Older Maria

Maria was cognizant of the challenges of attending college while having the responsibility of being a young mother to her two sons. As
her letter reveals, she was determined to pursue college, despite what
she may have felt in the past or what some may have told her about
how difficult life and school would be with two young children.
She was feeling like she could do well in college, especially since her
mother was watching her children while she attended school. But,
like the other CAMP students, she struggled in that transition, which

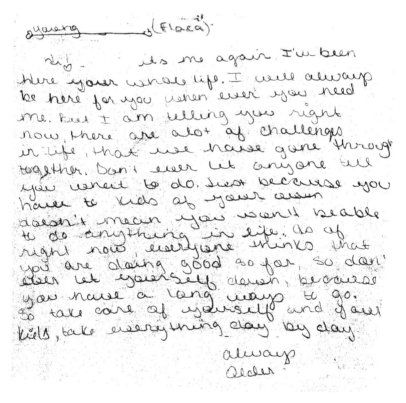

**Figure 2.3** Maria's letter to self.

is common in the crossing-over between communities of practice on and through the boundaries. In this process, according to Wenger (1998), the support provided by other members of the community of practice is key in the progress and survival of marginalized members like Maria initially making entry to the new community. Survival in the community and movement in the practice of being a successful student also depends on the response of the individual. The creation and evolution of identity in a community of practice is a negotiation. Maria's negotiation and navigation of her identity/ies was key to her movement toward learning to be a successful student in the CAMP community of practice. She was keenly aware that successfully navigating her way through her present life and schooling trajectory was not going to be easy (". . . there are a lot of challenges in life") and that it would be a long process ("you have a long ways to go"). Reflecting what Freire (1970) believes is necessary in order to transform one's life and situation, this realization may have helped her to learn how to become a better student. She confronted her present reality critically, realistically, concretely, and reflected on this in order to begin the transformation of what she knew was a complicated existence in her pursuit of an education.

## Concluding Thoughts on Maria's History

Maria's educational marginalization was amplified as a result of having to leave school due to her first pregnancy, to which a stigma is often attached in mainstream US schools. She left school feeling hopeless, with little desire to do anything, especially with the ridicule she received from her father. So she dropped out of school and enrolled in a GED program, which took her two years to complete. Although she struggled academically, Maria had the desire and willingness to learn in order to get an education, which she knew she needed to get a well-paying job. After having her children, she internalized discourses of being limited in her life and educational options, as evidenced in her "letter to self" that explicitly talked about how she could still do things in life despite having had children at a young age. Maria was determined and took advantage of the CAMP scholarship and exhibited good work ethics early on. Earlier in the year, her mother was able to watch her children while she attended class, participated in CAMP activities, and studied.

## Ruben: "Education wasn't about anything"

The expression of his jubilance was often disconcertingly loud, but it reflected a newfound happiness in his place in CAMP and college. Ruben, who labeled himself as Mexican and self-identified as a "cholo," a former Chicano gang member with a distinctive style of dress, speech, gestures, and/or tattoos (Vigil, 1988), was a short, stocky 21-year-old with a goatee, trimmed mustache, and glasses. When engaged in conversation, I felt the honesty in a truth he found in this newly forming sense of self as he started CAMP. It was as though he was speaking for the first time. But he was open with others about who he was in this world—a former gang member who wanted to change his ways. You could almost sense the war inside him about this desire. The conflicting identities. The battle between history and present determination. The basic urges to do and be something that did not involve violence, drugs, or a fight.

Born in San Pedro, California, Ruben was single and lived with his parents in a suburb of Denver at the time of this study. He had worked in warehouses, done agricultural field work, and worked in retail. His parents worked in canneries and agricultural fields, but his father did electrician's work at the time of this study. His mother was born in Yuba City, California, and his father was born in Mexico. He received his GED from a HEP CAMP (High School Equivalency Program–College Assistance Migrant Program) program near the community college where he attended CAMP. His ambition was to become a nurse, so that he could help people as had the many nurses who tended to him when he was physically wounded after gang fights and shootings.

Ruben had been in a gang most of his school life, from junior high through high school. His parents did not have much control over Ruben during high school, as he was almost always with his friends in the gang. His mother and father always pleaded with him to get out, though, and to go to school and become a better person. He rarely attended school during his high school years, and when he did, it was mostly to gather his friends from the gang to go out and sell drugs or just hang out. He expressed how to him "high school was a joke," admitting, "I did a lot of things I shouldn't have done."

Ruben did not have much of a formal schooling experience. He felt like he never belonged at school, indicating that he "didn't have a high school." He expressed how school at that time wasn't important, and that he never really needed it because he and his friends had to "make money." His gang life and what it represented ran Ruben's life, causing him to ignore other aspects of it. School was meaningless to Ruben. At such an early age, this activity on the streets and neglect of schoolwork contributed to his rapid adoption of cultural values and customs that shaped his identity as a gang member (Vigil, 1988). He said that "during high school, education wasn't about anything; it was about what you already knew. Even in junior high I gang-banged a little bit, from age 11-12 until the time I turned 19, I was hard-core cholo, didn't care about school, didn't care about anything. All I thought about was making that money, representing my 'hood.'"

Ruben eventually ended up in an alternative high school where he would show up at noon and work in an open and casual classroom environment at a pace with which he was comfortable. As long as he showed up for class, he did not have to go back to the juvenile detention center. He would go to class and work for a passing grade of a D. The great majority of his experiences with teachers as an adolescent were negative. There was a point, though, during his alternative school experience that Ruben felt a brief connection with a teacher. He appreciated the efforts of this teacher because of the positive environment that he created in his classroom. He said that teacher "*knew* [his emphasis] who was in his classroom. He wasn't *blinded* [his emphasis]. . . he didn't judge us for who we were, he believed every one of us had potential. I remember that first day . . . he goes, every one of you can be something 'cause I don't just see students, he goes, I see future presidents, military officers, he's all, doctors, lawyers, I don't see dead caskets. He goes, statistics say all you kids in my classroom are dead caskets. I don't see that." He admitted he never really listened to teachers before, but this one said something that appealed to him, especially coming from a white teacher. He never forgot what that teacher said to him, admitting, "It's always been with me. That's the one time I think that I've ever listened to a teacher. I don't remember anything teachers say. I never have until that one day . . . it kinda blew me out the water, you know. What even threw me off more was that he was white, working with a bunch of Mexicans in the community."

Ruben dropped out of high school when he moved to Colorado. He began working at a warehouse and eventually enrolled in a GED program, where he heard about the CAMP program and the possibility of attending college. Ruben suggested that he could have done more in his education before college, but does place some blame on high school and its system of informing and encouraging students to pursue college and postsecondary opportunities:

> They could have helped me with a lot more shit. Maybe it was the fact that they did, and I just didn't go. But maybe the counselors, I never had a counselor talk to me about going to college, or you know, you could get financial aid here to get, you know, I never had any of that during high school. So I mean, that might have helped maybe, and maybe if I—and I can't really blame it all on the school either you know—'cause maybe if I would have went to school more, I would have been in college a whole long time ago. I mean I'm not gonna blame the school saying that's why I didn't go to college, 'cause I didn't go to college 'cause that was my choice, at the time.

Ruben struggled in his transition into college on a number of levels. He had to work a lot to help with the family finances. Academically, Ruben entered college through the CAMP program with inadequate preparation for college. Table 2.5 shows his Accuplacer test scores.

TABLE 2.5. Ruben's Accuplacer Scores

| Accuplacer Test | Score |
| --- | --- |
| Reading comprehension | 68 |
| Sentence skills | 62 |
| Elementary algebra | 29 |
| Arithmetic | 45 |

Ruben's scores placed him in ENG 060–Writing Fundamentals and MAT 060–Pre-Algebra, which were developmental courses for which he would not receive college credit. He took college-level courses in the learning communities and Adventure Learning/P.E. classes that were required by the CAMP program.

## Concluding Thoughts on Ruben's History

Ruben came from very little schooling experience, admitting that he often ditched class and eventually dropped out. And any school or classroom experience he had was often lacking rigor or high expectations in academic achievement. Ruben's history of schooling experience in such settings contrasted with the more structured and rigorous academic settings that typically define college coursework and classroom participation. There were also high family expectations to contribute to the family finances, which forced him to commit to jobs that would meet those needs and ultimately conflict with his schooling schedule.

Ruben's social and educational marginalization stemmed from his gang activity and the disconnect that this created between him and school. He was also socioeconomically marginalized, having lived in government project housing, with his parents working low-paying jobs. Ruben also was perceived as "not caring" about school, most of his teachers reciprocating that attitude and telling Ruben and others like him that they were "statistics," until he entered alternative school. At one point in his schooling, there was a teacher who showed Ruben the possibilities in the positive teaching and learning that can occur between teacher and student. And Ruben remembered this. In his formative years, Ruben never participated in a community of students that engaged in the practice of what it was to be and become successful students. His cultural and historical experience and learning did not create a space for a student identity that would otherwise feel comfortable and capable of dealing with the challenges of college life and academics.

Before, Ruben was accustomed to committing to one identity— that of being in a gang and being a cholo gangbanger. He had been isolated and estranged from his family. School and doing schoolwork had never been a priority. He was committed to being and becoming one identity within his gang and peer culture. Enacting that one identity was in contrast to the multiple identities he had to enact while in college through the CAMP program. This was the beginning of the contentious nature of his experience and identity formation in his first year of college and CAMP.

## Community Boundaries,
## Beginning New Identities: Transition

Freire (1970) believed that in reaching a certain level of consciousness, "the oppressed must confront reality critically, simultaneously objectifying and acting upon that reality. A mere perception of reality not followed by this critical intervention will not lead to a transformation of objective reality—precisely because it is not a true perception" (p.52). In reflecting on their past schooling and life experiences as they entered and began experiencing college through CAMP, each student *named*, confronted, and was consciously aware of what contributed to his or her past and present marginalization. This movement toward a new level of consciousness reveals the students understanding that individual choice, reflection, and action for change clashed with the grander oppressive ideologies that did not make life any easier for students like them, the marginalized. But in moving toward this level of awareness, they realized they had choice. And there was great power in this choice at this moment of their lives.

The CAMP students embodied a resilience that has brought them to this place of awareness, desire, and the beginning of college. Resilient students are those who invoke a "reality check" (McMillan and Reed, 1994) in which they reflect on their world and current position within that world. Freire (1970) knew this process well and knew that further steps are necessary in the path toward consciousness, what he called praxis—"reflection and action upon the world in order to transform it" (p. 51). The students must have engaged in this reflection at some point in their lives to come to a state of consciousness that made them realize more about their current life situations, and what they needed to do in order to change them. Was it before the CAMP experience? Or was their praxis triggered by the presence and possibility of a CAMP scholarship and the impact that could have on them? We will not know for sure, but we do know that they have chosen to be resilient in the past, as now. Their resilience has brought them here.

Reflected in many of their stories of schooling, the CAMP students have internalized the deficit perspectives and pedagogy rooted in the broader social and educational structures that have created inequitable schooling. But they also remembered the individuals who planted within them the knowledge that, indeed, there are people who care. They have been influenced by their familial, teacher, peer, and broader social networks. And, of course, as within all families, cultures, and peer and social networks, there will always be supportive and unsupportive influences. The influences are near and distant. Present and historic. These interactions with particular individuals—parents, teachers, friends, relatives—are ones that the CAMP students carry with them. They even recall those cursory relationships in schools that are so prominent in today's vast schools and overcrowded classrooms. A memory, emotion, bit of knowledge, or slight understanding must have been planted. They have identified, named, and recognized the intersection of realities that brought them to this level of consciousness; that all of these micro and macro interactional dynamics have brought them to this place in their lives and education. And perhaps this has begun their movement from a marginal existence.

# 3

## College through CAMP

### Access, Community, and Opportunity to Learn

THERE ARE STILL PROBLEMS in providing access and opportunities for marginalized Mexican American students (Gándara and Contreras, 2009). And even if they are provided with access to particular communities of practice, often the practice within those communities is disconnected from the social and academic networks that could provide students with the necessary cultural and academic capital necessary to thrive in a complex web of social and schooling contexts (Stanton-Salazar, 2001; Tinto, 1993). When provided with access to the social, cultural, personal, and academic networks in college that lead to relationships with faculty, staff, and peers, students thrive and persist (Pascarella and Terenzini, 1991, 2005). Furthermore, studies show that the influence and learning that come from social and academic support networks do not have to be extensive and complicated to contribute to student success. They begin as very localized and intimate. At the high-school level, for example, a migrant student club serves as a community within the larger community of high school (Gibson, Bejínez, Hidalgo, and Rolón, 2004). It is a place where students could enact a common discourse, practice a student identity that engages their history of language and culture and not feel misplaced or stigmatized. They could be students while being Mexican and migrant at the same time. Such spaces within the vastness of school and schooling are essential to the retention of marginalized Mexican American students, at all levels of schooling. It is a space that resembles that of a family.

Woven throughout the CAMP program were numerous spaces that created a family-like network with members that counted on each other for personal and academic support. These spaces were part of a larger program design that considered not only the need for building community, relationships, and trust in one another, but learning and understanding the pragmatics of academic and college-going persistence. The CAMP program design and philosophy recognized the importance of weaving together the practical with the passionate in teaching and learning for student success.

CAMP encompassed a number of courses, events, workshops, and other programmatic characteristics that provided various forms of support. The beginning of the school year consisted of orientations and meetings in which students would gain practical knowledge and insight about registering for classes, applying for financial aid, and learning good study habits. At some of these same orientations there would be motivational guest speakers who also served as role models for the students. Some of the courses were offered as learning communities in which the entire cohort of CAMP students would take two common courses together, such as English and Freshman Seminar. In these classes, guest speakers were frequently invited to address various topics related to the students' lives. Students then wrote papers or did projects based on what they gleaned from the speakers. These courses were often team-taught by instructors who were readily available to assist the students not only with their academics, but with personal issues as well.

Another part of the curriculum was the Adventure Learning course. In this course the students learned about trust and building community, but they also learned problem-solving skills and practiced their writing. Outside of the regular curriculum, the CAMP program also provided tutoring services, field trips, financial aid guidance, and counseling on planning for the next academic year as well as postgraduate academic and professional opportunities.

The CAMP community of practice was a network comprised of invested individuals who cared about student success. Available to address the academic and the personal were the CAMP coordinator, recruiter, and counselors, usually found in a student lounge in the building where the CAMP office was located. These CAMP officials took on many roles to meet the needs of the students. It was not uncommon to see a CAMP student sitting and crying with the CAMP coordinator after a long day of classes. The lounge was often the place where CAMP students congregated, tutored one another, or just commiserated. There was also the CAMP Cyber Mentor Project, in which students were mentored by individuals experienced as college students, many with professional and advanced degrees, and Latino like the students. Principally via e-mail communication, mentors provided guidance, wisdom, and practical advice on succeeding in college.

This authentic caring went beyond superficialities and simple acknowledgment of one another's presence in the school or classroom (Noddings, 1992; Valenzuela, 1999). It was reflected in the willingness of CAMP staff, college instructors, and mentors to be present often, to offer personal and academic advice, and to be genuine. In a well-functioning community of practice, student success, radical new insights, and the creation of knowledge require a strong, communal bond and a respect for all experiences, good and bad (Wenger, 1998). For the CAMP students, validating such experience and its value in teaching and learning was shown in the various forms of support that acknowledged the students' history and humanness.

Peers and peer networks were also vital in student success. They are very powerful in schooling. Gibson, Gándara, and Koyama (2004) present a number of examples of how peer networks can contribute to the creation of a positive academic trajectory but also at times be detrimental. Peer networks are also delicate but can be managed to create surprising results in the goal of student academic success. In the CAMP community of practice, for example, peer networks were purposely developed in the Adventure Learning and learning community courses in which the entire CAMP cohort took classes together. Students gravitated to one another in times of need. They sometimes disagreed, and not all students got along at all times, as in any family. But the students knew that they could count on a human presence throughout their first-year college experience. This peer network within CAMP contributed to the maintenance of personal and academic well-being.

The CAMP program components, curriculum, and interactional dynamics affected in numerous ways how the students participated in courses, committed to their studies, juggled responsibilities, became empowered, and ultimately saw themselves as developing college students. It was a process that began with the students understanding the significance of their entry into the CAMP and college community of practice by winning the scholarship. It continued with their understanding of how vital their active participation through practice, presence, and internalization of their experience was to their learning and understanding in the movement toward learning how to be a successful student. The students acknowledged the powerful role of others within the CAMP community—from invested individuals to those in their peer network—in this process too.

## Change in Life and Schooling Trajectory

Based on Lave and Wenger's (1991) view of learning and learning identity within a community of practice, learning and development begin in the movement away from a marginalized space. This begins with access to this community, to resources, and to its members, along with opportunities to practice. For many of the CAMP students, experiencing college through the CAMP program was entry to a new path in life. It was access to a community of practice with others who were engaging in work and struggle to be and become something new and different, and to learn. It was an opportunity to have a schooling experience that many CAMP students had thought inaccessible because of their past academic performance, preconceived beliefs about only certain "types" being accepted in college, or lack of resources for it, financial or otherwise.

For Laura, the CAMP experience was about making up for lost time in school. Because she left high school in early ninth grade, she never thought she would be in a position to attend college and get a scholarship like CAMP offered. She said that this experience "showed me that I guess I can have a second chance and that there's a program out there that can help people. That wants you to try to succeed. To want to push you to having a better job, better life for yourself and your family." This past year was a time and place for

Laura to see what she could accomplish. It was an opportunity for her to test her abilities in school, and whether she could accomplish what goals she set in front of her. It allowed her to prove to herself "I can do it, that it's not just myself that did it, but I helped myself out and it was the CAMP program that helped me to get started. The CAMP scholarship and the CAMP Program. Just that I could do anything that I could set my mind to." As Laura suggests here, the practice of being in the CAMP program and having the opportunity to "get started" in learning how to be a successful student fueled her aspirations to complete college. Simply being in and remaining in school, something Laura did not do in high school, positively influences academic aspirations. Laura's being in and remaining in the CAMP program within a supportive community reflects how a sense of belonging is an important factor in engagement in school, which is linked to a desire to do well academically (Gándara, O'Hara, and Gutiérrez, 2004).

Cristina felt an experience like this one could lead her to other opportunities in life. It was a chance for her to prove to herself and others that she could be a successful student. She felt like CAMP was "just one door, just somebody . . . Lisa [the CAMP coordinator] doesn't realize this is just her job, but she doesn't realize how she impacts a student's life and how she makes a change. Because of her, my life could be changed for the rest of my life. So, I just think one door, one opportunity, one chance, you know? And actually, giving me a chance, and that made me also believe in myself, and that's why I'm here."

Luz saw the CAMP program as a chance to understand the nature of college, and what would be required of her as a person and student to reach her goal of becoming a nurse. She said that "in starting college, it helped me learn what it is to be in college. It gave me a head start, to prepare, how to get prepared for going to a university and getting my degree." Luz worked very hard to succeed in high school, which she continued to do in college. By engaging in that practice of working hard, she quickly realized that "doing college" was possible and she would be able to reach her goals. It was a chance to test her work ethic in higher education, which the CAMP scholarship and experience allowed her to do.

Ruben learned from his successes, but mostly from his failures to commit to certain requirements of the program. This experience showed him what he needed to know in order to succeed, which fueled his agency and provided life direction. This scholarship and opportunity was what he needed to learn more about himself and his capabilities.

> No matter what, I know that I can make it. That's what I learned from CAMP. All the struggles and all that, if I really didn't want it, I wouldn't have come to class all those times. I wouldn't have shown up today if I didn't care. Before, if I didn't care, I wouldn't have shown up. Guaranteed, if this was two years ago, if I didn't want it, I wouldn't have been here. Yeah, I screwed up, I did some things I shouldn't have done. I should have kept my head on straight at school and classes, but I can't. Maybe this is just my foot in the door. My teaching, my learning, my lesson, on what *not to do*. I think maybe some people, what they need is that lesson. Give those people a lesson on what not to do. This is my first year to learn what to do and what not to do. That's how it works, for everybody.

Ruben did not attend many of his classes. But he attended more classes and participated in more school than he would have had he not been a part of a community like CAMP in college. Ruben felt that his "trying to be here, trying to come here, trying to make it" made him realize what was possible. For Ruben, the CAMP experience was an entry point to a place where he could at least try to be a college student, allowed to perform and engage as who and what he was at that moment with his own knowledge and skills. This was a chance for him to learn how to care for school, and to attach meaning to it. In this community of practice, Ruben moved beyond his marginal existence to a place in his learning trajectory, a place where he "showed up," that took him closer to realizing something or somebody different.

The CAMP experience also allowed students to engage in various activities with other students of the program, as well as with staff, instructors, and community members, that contributed to a sense of community. The participation in such activities helped students to first recognize their role in this community and enact a sensibility of who they needed to be and become in order to participate fully within this community. In this participation, they practiced to become more knowledgeable students, while accepting and following the guidance and apprenticing of the staff, instructors, and others involved.

The CAMP orientation day is an integral part of the CAMP program design and the launching point into the college experience. One day before she began her first day of college through the CAMP program, Cristina remembered how grateful she felt for the scholarship and all that the program was about during orientation. To have all the instructors, staff, and CAMP personnel present, introducing themselves and their services to the students, made Cristina feel welcomed and a part of a network of resources to ensure her academic and personal success. She said, "It inspired me into doing a great job, because it wasn't just pay for your college, it's like, we're a team, we're a group, we're a class [cohort]. . . . I think the orientation made me feel like, because it was the beginning, and I didn't know them . . . it made me feel like I did want to be dedicated, because all these things they told me about how they were going to help me out and stuff." Cristina felt like others were invested in her, so she should commit herself fully to the cause of being a good student. She was encouraged and empowered by people from the college who had that interest in her as a student and wanted to see her succeed.

## Elements of Community

### Adventure Learning Classes

Learning to build trust, open communication, and working together as a family unit was a key goal of the activities of the Adventure Learning classes. These activities created situations in which students had to interact to learn about one another, build trust, and practice teamwork. Many of the students were able to build strong relationships with other students in the cohort, creating relationships of personal, academic, and even financial support (because of lack of money to pay rent, some students lived with others at certain times throughout the academic year). There were many activities in the Adventure Learning courses that engaged the students in teamwork and trust-building activities, such as a ropes course or small-group problem-solving discussions related to life issues. Below are reconstructed field notes that illustrate an activity that allowed students to participate in a manner that had few restrictions on expression of the self, building trust, and learning from one another.

> The students, along with the coordinator, recruiter and myself, have been playing balloon games all morning. I am presently observing the games. There are several small groups of three or four students sitting in a circle using their hands to prevent a balloon from touching the floor. The main goal is to work as a team to achieve this goal. Alicia, the instructor for the Adventure Learning course, suddenly tells the group, "Challenge to you!" and instructs the students to sit up with their knees propped up to a point where the person in front of them can lean on them, and creating a small group circle. They still have to prevent the balloon from touching the ground. The students are following directions well for this game. Most of the balloons have not touched the floor. I hear one group of four girls near me directing each other to "bump the balloon to the middle" of their circle and to "keep on each other's back," referring to keeping their circle intact, although they can't really see each other very well from the way they are positioned. Alicia yells to all the groups, "You've gotta trust the person behind you!" She continues to tell them that it is a game of "blind trust" and that "developing trust takes time." She concludes the game by telling them that "we learn as a group—if we can learn to lean on each other, to move together is different and it takes work and trust."

For Cristina, the Adventure Learning course (taken for physical education credit) helped her learn to be more trusting of others, to be herself more, allowing some of her expressive identity to unleash itself, and to feel comfortable within the CAMP community. She admitted that she was naturally shy and would avoid being the center of attention, but after having engaged in Adventure Learning, she said "But now, I got to trust everybody and we got to know everybody, and in my class I started losing that shyness and now I can speak out.

It's okay if I stutter and stuff like that, you've got to trust people. So that's what I learned, how to not be shy, and to try and speak out."

Ruben suggested that the Adventure Learning course made the cohort closer and he was able to bond with people with whom he would not have bonded in the past:

> I think that was good because it brought the CAMP students together. And that's when you realize who you can lean . . . your head on their shoulder. And who you can't. To me, that gave me two homeboys who gave me a backbone. If I needed something, Bobby (a friend from the CAMP cohort) was there, and I learned that. Those activities that Alicia had, you had to build a lot of trust, and I was willing to give, and where I come from, you don't trust nobody. You can't trust nobody but yourself. Because you couldn't.

Ruben made new friends but also learned how to trust people, something he was unable to do in the past.

Laura admitted that the Adventure Learning course helped her tremendously in interacting and communicating with others. She realized it would help in her college career "because there was a lot of teamwork and communicating. Communication is so important in college, because if you have a question and you don't ask, you'll never get anywhere. You can try to find out yourself, but it will be too hard, it's easier to ask." Laura expressed an awareness of the need to interact with the outside world in order to survive and succeed. She realized that there are ways to tap into people and social networks in order to learn. Being a part of the CAMP community for Laura meant that she felt valued being a part of something that allowed her to be more open and be herself. She found comfort in the fact that "they'll talk to you, they care about you. Everybody's real nice. Just a big family, almost. I guess it made me feel comfortable. I can talk to them, even if I don't talk much."

When Maria went on the Adventure Learning course in the mountain retreat and camping trip, it also allowed her to be comfortable in her own skin. She said, "I learned to be more open, not to keep everything to myself, because that's how I was in high school. I learned a lot by going out with the students, to be around them, not to be so shy and to hold everything back." The opportunity also gave her the chance to practice another aspect of her identity, one that had been hidden for so long. She was able to share more of who she was.

For many students in this study, interacting with others in various experiences helped them to learn to go out of their comfort zone. Luz told me that participating in the Adventure Learning course influenced her to take more risks, and to do things she wasn't able to do much during her childhood.

> Usually I'm afraid to do stuff. In dealing with school, I would say I can't do things. But that class showed me it's okay to take risks. The activities made me feel like a little kid again. When I was a little girl, I didn't really play as much as I would like. I couldn't play because I was working in the fields very young. I started when I was probably nine, but before that, I would have to clean the house and other chores. My sisters would always yell at me. I had to work and had no opportunities for play. My parents didn't want us to be outside playing. They didn't want people to be seeing us playing and think that we wouldn't do anything in the house.

Luz felt as if she lost a part of her childhood to obligations of work to her family. For many migrant children, helping with household chores and working in the field alongside their parents becomes a normal part of their youth, and is so out of economic necessity and survival (Green, 2003; Olsen and Jaramillo, 1999; Salerno, 1991). And, like Luz, migrant children may miss out on the simplicity of youthful play. Luz lived a life not knowing much outside of work to help contribute to family finances and aid in the daily quest to survive. She grew up being "afraid to do stuff," inside and outside of school. In CAMP, what appeared as activities for group bonding and testing physical abilities and problem-solving skills in their Adventure Learning course turned out to be an opportunity for reliving a part of a childhood that Luz rarely experienced. It was an experience that allowed for the emergence of a youthful and more confident self who discovered that it was "okay to take risks."

## Learning Community Classes

For Maria, the CAMP community helped her to focus on her school-work and understand her roles and responsibilities as a college student. Participating in learning community classes was a time when the CAMP students had a class as a cohort and functioned as one unit. In the learning community class, they tended to hold one another responsible academically. It was not only an academic system of support, but a social one within the CAMP community of practice. In thinking about the learning communities courses, Maria felt more invested in her education and aware of her actions as a student because of the accountability system that was emphasized to the students within these courses.

> I've learned a lot being here; in high school I didn't learn that much; but when I'm here, it seems like I pay more attention. I'm worried about everything that I do, making sure that I have all my work done and everything like that. I'm more cautious now than before, and I think that has helped me a lot. To be, not prepared, but to be right there, to be able to do my work and understand everything that I have to do with CAMP. Before, I didn't care, and now I do. I see things differently from what I did before.

The learning communities created in their academic courses gave Maria a sense of perspective in her role as student. Maria's situation and experience here illustrates Wenger's (1998) idea that identity is both a process and a place that offers an alternative form of participation. This was different from her past, which was essentially non-participation when she had her children and was out of school. In this new practice of being a student, Maria's simple presence in an academic community was a major accomplishment. This presence carried much more meaning for her than the actual engagement of work in the practice of being a student at the time. As for many of the other CAMP participants, access and presence were seminal in the beginning of their trajectory, practice, learning, and change.

The following reconstructed field notes are an illustration of how the learning community course provided a context for the students to not only engage in discussion and actions of accountability among themselves, but also with members of the broader community. In this case, the instructors of a learning community (psychology and Master Student) course brought in a guest speaker to dialogue with the students on her own personal experiences in college, and what they could do to overcome obstacles. Ruben's participation is highlighted in this illustration.

Today they (instructors James and Cinthia) bring in a guest speaker, Suny Urrutia Moore. She is featured in the Master Student textbook as the winner of an essay contest in which the participants wrote essays about their learning to become a master student. Cinthia invited her to speak to the students on issues of dedication, motivation, and good study habits, also because she is uniquely featured in the book and was also a student once at Next Step Community College. She is originally from Chile, South America, where she had done work as an accountant. She speaks of the importance and need to learn English well to the students, and answers a number of questions from the students about her life as a student and as a mother and the various challenges that went along with taking on school while dealing with other challenges of life. The students ask her questions about coming to the United States from Chile and how she adjusted. She tells them that it was culture shock at first, but told them how it was "very helpful to get out because it helped me learn English." She tells them how the education system is different in the United States than in Chile. She recalls how in Chile "they didn't teach me how to learn. They always make us memorize and regurgitate." She told them that the Master Student class helped her to learn how to learn.

Suny tells them that one of her motivations to going to college was that she "always felt a step behind" in life and was "insecure about her writing skills" and her academic capabilities. She says that she "wanted to do it for myself to make me feel better." She tells them that she wants to be successful, which, to her, means "being able to make a difference in someone's life."

One student, Ruben, asks her about the study techniques that she enjoys and that have helped her the most. She admits that the memorization techniques were very helpful to her, using 3 × 5 note cards throughout her years of study. She says that "trying to keep yourself awake and very active is important" and goes on by telling them that using various tools like markers and pens, writing notes in notebooks, and studying when your mind is fresh are crucial things to know. She mentions that "delegating your time and learning time management skills" is also very important, which meant that she had to show her children how to make their own lunches for school and get supper started, when she couldn't be there to do that for them.

She works as a literacy advocate for migrant families but tells the students that her goal is to finish her bachelor's degree and teach Spanish or ESL, or possibly work as a court interpreter.

A Latina student asks Suny if "her family ever gave up" on her. Suny admits that some things, such as a social life, do suffer some, but would make her family and children a part of her goals in education and teach them what she was learning being a student. She tells the students that she has taught her children values and morals and study and life skills.

One of the last things she tells the students, when a white, male student asks about motivation to do her work and all that is required to being a student, what he calls giving oneself a "pep talk," she simply replies that she just "makes the decision to do it and stick with it." She tells the class that she "struggled with not believing in myself," because even though she thought she had good academic skills when she began, she discovered it was more difficult than she thought. She says she was overwhelmed, but winning something like the essay contest boosted her confidence and made her feel better.

A white, female student finally asks her how she handled the anxiety of tests and academics, and Suny replies, "I did what it took to do well; once you prepare, the anxiety will disappear; you put in the time and you will be ready."

The learning community course often provided opportunities for the students to gain insight into the lives of others who had experienced what they were currently experiencing in school. This aspect of being in a community of practice illustrated the importance of time and practice and amplified for the students the importance of "person in history" and one who has "been there, done that" and succeeded. This brought the history of others into their present schooling experience. Suny became a part of their community of practice to be and become a successful student by contributing to their sense of history and possibility in the midst of their struggle and experience. She was a living example of what was and what could be for the students.

## Invested Others and People Who Care

A number of "invested others" were involved in the implementation and operation of the CAMP program. These "invested others" were individuals who played a key role in the personal and academic support of the students throughout the academic year and invested their time and energy at various levels of involvement. In a community of practice, these invested others, who are often more knowledgeable and have more experience, are vital in the learning process. As Rendón (1994) found early in her study of nontraditional students in their first year of college, these invested others (or what she called agents, or what González, Stoner, and Jovel (2003) called agents of social capital) are especially important in helping students to visualize their success. She learned that both in-class and out-of-class validation provided the needed interactions for such students to learn confidence in doing college academic work, and the agency needed to continue despite obstacles. In this dynamic, the acceptance of more knowledgeable others and the interactions they have with the CAMP students legitimizes their participation and learning. The learner feels valued in the community as a novice (Lave and Wenger, 1991).

Invested others are named as such because of the roles they played outside of the fixed and planned curriculum, having more flexible and ubiquitous identities as ones who invested themselves and the skills and knowledge they had to offer at that moment of need for the students. "Invested others" also stems from the notion that these individuals were genuinely interested and invested in the lives of these students and their success. Invested others included CAMP staff, instructors, and individuals who mentored the students via cyberspace (e-mail), called cyber mentors. There were two levels of support for the students that the invested others provided: personal support and academic support.

## Personal Support

Angie, the CAMP recruiter, suggested that the notion of showing genuine interest in the well-being of the students contributed to the approachability and effectiveness of the CAMP staff and instructors and may have contributed to student learning and success.

> Them interacting with us, it kind of felt like a comfortable place to go. . . . They've gotten to know us the most, and I think that with them having so many different options, and they know kind of how we all react to different things, has been able to give them a chance to decide who they think they should tell their problems to, or who they think they need to talk to about certain situations. And I think it's kind of helped their success rate, only because they know that we're doing it just out of the goodness of our hearts, we're not trying to do anything on our part to keep our jobs or anything like that. We're doing it because we honestly care. What I've heard is that they feel like they're real comfortable with us, so if they do run into a problem, they'd rather come to us instead of some of the other Next Step personnel, which is good, because when you run into problems in college, you don't always know where the resources are to do that. That's kind of what I've gotten from the students.

Although having acknowledged that he did not perform up to the college and CAMP's standards, Ruben said that he would have performed far worse than he did had he not been a part of something like CAMP. With all the coursework, family pressures, and financial obligations, the people in the program and the relationships he had with particular individuals made the difference for him. He said that peers in the CAMP cohort were essential to his participation, suggesting, "I would have been gone within the first half of the quarter. If it weren't for Bobby, I wouldn't have even been here most of the time. It was just, oh my God, guaranteed, if I was like that the first year, by myself, oh no. I would have gotten frustrated, everything at my house would have gone down, I wouldn't have a homeboy to calm me down when shit got heated. Things would have turned out a whole lot differently, I know it."

In Ruben's times of struggle throughout the year, he mentioned how the coordinator, Lisa, was also a presence that made him think about his actions, decisions, and routes in life. Below is a vignette constructed from field notes on a time when I observed Ruben getting counsel from Lisa.

> I look over the half-wall of Lisa's cubicle office and see Lisa talking to Ruben in her office in the student lounge. Ruben is whispering to her rapidly, looking stressed about some situation that I cannot make out. He looks up at me and appears to want privacy while talking to her about this situation. Lisa also looks concerned. I turn away and think about how I often see Lisa working with students on an individual basis. This isn't the first time I hear of Lisa counseling Ruben, either. She often tells me about how much she has to talk to Ruben about his personal, family, and financial issues. Ruben is having many problems, and it seems to be affecting his school work.

Ruben's personal finances and outside responsibilities were continuing to weigh down his efforts in college, as was the lure of his past money-making activities. Whatever Lisa would tell him, it would make him reconsider.

> When I have some intense problems, I'll talk to her about them, or when I think I can't hang with it anymore, sometimes I feel like just quitting. I'll talk to her, because she always makes you think twice. There was a time I told her I thought I was going to quit. I don't think I can do college anymore. And she said, no, no, no, just stick with it, you can do it. So I say, okay, I'll try again, I'll try. She gives you that extra push sometimes that you need.

The CAMP coordinator, Lisa, was present in almost every aspect of the CAMP students' lives. She was present at the meetings, sometimes in their classes, and always in her office to be accessible to the students. Cristina said that the CAMP coordinator was the most helpful in her first-year college experience, having demanded excellence from her but also having provided comfort and understanding through a personal relationship:

> Lisa's the one who has helped me the most. She wants a lot. She knows I could go very far, and she wants a lot from me. She has helped me in every way . . . she cheered me on and I could tell her everything. Lisa and Cinthia, Cinthia has been the teacher who has helped me succeed, and Lisa's the one cheering me on and telling me, "Go do this, go do that!" and I know she wants a lot from me in my life, and she knows I can go very far. I think we get along and communicate really well. She was a great motivator to go to college.

Luz was always battling the fear of romance and a relationship taking her away from her pursuits. Luz mentioned that she has always had confidence in her academic abilities, mainly because of the encouragement she received from her parents and from so many teachers. This academic trajectory was often fed through support and interactions with instructors such as Cinthia, who were especially invested in the CAMP program philosophy. She often affirmed her identity as a strong student with their availability throughout the CAMP program. This allowed Luz to continue to feel confident in what she was doing academically. She said, "I guess it's all the compliments from my teachers over the years. That I did well, that I was smart, all the way through school. Even this past year in college. Like Cinthia, she would say that I wrote good essays. I had heard that before, too. So that reinforces me. If I know how to write, then I can get other things done."

Laura mentioned how her first two instructors in college from the learning community were very helpful in providing support, academic and personal. She said that their accessibility was key in helping her to succeed in her first quarter in college. Laura told me, "They're just always there for you, to help you, if you have questions, they'll answer them." One instructor in particular helped Laura overcome many of her fears and struggles. She said that Cinthia "helped me a lot with writing. She helped me get less stressed out. She told me to calm down, 'It's okay, it won't be like this forever, the class will end.' She talked with me personally about stuff. She has to talk in front of crowds, she'd get real nervous, almost faint, kind of like how I felt." The constant presence of more knowledgeable others and their ability to empathize with students helped students deal with the challenges of their coursework, personal issues, and everyday life. This feature of the CAMP community of practice illustrated that apprenticing the CAMP students from their peripheral practice was a necessary dynamic in their learning, at least early on. Because once the students develop more independent practice, a goal of communities of practice, this level of support is slowly minimized (Lave and Wenger, 1991; Wenger, 1998; Vygotsky, 1978).

## Cyber Support

Another aspect of the CAMP program was mentoring support through e-mail correspondence. For marginalized Latino students in college, mentors can be a source of personal, academic, and general support that contributes to their academic motivation and success (Campos et al., 2009). Students were paired with a member of the college or university to provide various forms of encouragement and support. Laura was comforted by the thought of having another person in her support network in cyberspace through the Cyber Mentor Project. She thought it was helpful personally and academically for her to know "someone else, you know, to talk to like a friend like another person to help me out and give me advice so . . . that was good." Below is an example of the type of correspondence that occurred between Laura and her cyber mentor, who provided useful career and further educational information.

Hi Elisabeth,

How are you doing? Our reaction papers and our presentations were suppose [*sic*] to be due today but now they will be due on Monday, because we are going to look at our Myers-Briggs Type Indicator test its just a sort of personality test. I took that test last quarter for career planning class. Some of the camp students didn't like it because they thought it was wrong.

I thought it was good because I think it pretty much summed up what kind of personality I have.

How was your weekend? Did you have a fun time at the party?

In my English class we are starting to revise our essays. This class is hard. Its [*sic*] a lot of work. Monday I took a test in math and I got a 95 percent. I was so happy that I got that high of a score because some of the math concepts were a little confusing. I had to study proportions, ratios, and percents.

Thank you for your support,

Laura

Laura and her cyber mentor had recently visited at a pizza party organized by the CAMP program. Laura gave her mentor a gift, talked more about her future plans, and showed off her boyfriend.

The cyber mentor was often a source of advice and information. In the following response to Laura's last e-mail, Elisabeh refers her to a website that has information about a school that has programs for people interested in veterinary medicine, something Laura had mentioned she would like to study. The mentor follows with words of encouragement and support for Laura's efforts in school.

Hi Laura! Thank you for the cute dog! I love stuffed animals. It now has a home with my other cuddly animals. It was great to visit with you and your boyfriend. I had a lot of fun, especially when you got an award for your awesome grades. You are doing so well in school. About school, I saw a commercial about a school that has a vet. tech program. It's called Bel-Rea Institute and the website is (www.bel-rea.com). They have internships and scholarships that you should look into. This is from the website: Located at the base of the Rocky Mountains in beautiful Colorado, Bel-Rea Institute of Animal Technology is one of the largest veterinary technician schools in the United States. It might be something that you might consider. It looks like there are some jobs available throughout Colorado.

Wow! That is fantastic getting a 95 percent on your math test. You never know, math might be your favorite subject once you're finished with school. How did your presentation go today? Are you working on any other big projects?

Take care,

Elisabeth

Laura thought the Cyber Mentor Project was good for her, to know that someone was available to provide insight to going through college. She said her mentor acted as "another link to someone that's gone through college, another friend . . . another person there for you."

The Cyber Mentor Project was also a positive force in Ruben's life. He talked about how the few interactions with his mentor encouraged him to fight through the adversity he was experiencing in school and that there was hope through his struggle. He mentioned how he valued what his mentor had to tell him: "He gave me advice. He told me, people and things might seem like they are holding you down and bringing you down, but don't let them, always fight them . . . when he does give advice, it's good advice. When I need it, in a time of frustration, he gives it."

## People Who Care

Reflecting Noddings's (1992) and Valenzuela's (1999) notion of caring, Laura remembered the people and staff in the CAMP program as an integral part of her comfort and success in school. The positive environment created by the goals and activities of the program allowed her to progress through school without having to worry about subtractive relationships or people:

> I guess everybody in general was nice and supportive. Nobody's saying you can't do it or you're not going past the first quarter, anything like that, everybody's real nice and supportive and that helped build a good atmosphere because . . . I can't think of anyone who wasn't supportive. Everybody was. . . . Nobody was mean or hateful. It showed me that there are people who actually do care and want to see you succeed. I think back in high school, I didn't feel cared about, and teachers didn't care, they just wanted you to come to class, do the work, and turn it

in. That's it. I didn't feel that back then, but now in the CAMP
Program, it felt like a real caring atmosphere with the people
there.

Luz was also encouraged by the positive support and caring attitudes of teachers from her past and from the CAMP program.
Suggesting the power of the encouragement from her teachers and
adults invested in her academic endeavors, Luz expressed that "if
they wouldn't have given me any compliments or suggestions, then
I would feel like they didn't care about me, or that I don't exist."
Luz also mentioned how helpful her cyber mentor was in their correspondence. Earlier in the year her mentor had given her blunt advice
about staying in an English class that Luz didn't like and that she
should "get over it" and that "she could do it." Luz responded well
to this approach to advice giving, and stated that her mentor had
always given her advice about school through their correspondence:
"It makes me feel like she really cares, really wants to know."

Ruben remembered James (psychology instructor) and William
(English instructor) always being positive forces for him throughout
the year. Ruben thought these types of teachers existed only in mov-
ies and could not really be like that for someone like him:

> That was just weird. Because where I came from, teachers
> don't care where I come from. I've read stories, I've watched
> movies, *Stand and Deliver, Dangerous Minds,* you know, that
> one teacher who cares about whether their students make it
> or not. I've never seen one of those except for Ted [former
> alternative high school teacher], but it was different with Ted,
> because that was high school, and still in high school I didn't
> care about teachers. But he was always cool [James]. James
> came up and said, "You can make it." So did William. William
> read my stuff, and he was like, "Ruben, how come you don't
> turn this stuff in, man? Look at your essay, how come you
> don't turn it in to me?" But coming here, it was different, be-
> cause people cared. They wanted to see us graduate and make
> it, and that was different for me. That was really different, for
> where I come from, teachers lack emotion. . . . "You're a sta-
> tistic. There's my paycheck whether you come or go." Because

I had a teacher tell me that. "You're a statistic, whether you come or go, I still get my paycheck."

Ruben suggests that the teachers who have had the most impact on him are those who expressed a sense of "emotion" in their pedagogy, in their interactions with him. These teachers in the CAMP program were key in motivating him to continue on his path toward learning how to be a successful student. And even though he had a teacher in high school who reflected some sense of caring in his pedagogy, Ruben admitted at the time he still "didn't care about teachers." One of the main differences between the community of practice in high school and that of CAMP lay in the trajectories of the students surrounding him. He was in an alternative schooling program in high school, where students tended to be less motivated to do well in school. In CAMP, all the students were in a culture and community of practice that was driven by change, learning, hard work, and determination to do well in school and in life. Perhaps that is why Ruben cared more now in CAMP than he did in high school. Could such a community of practice have been created in high school to change his uncaring attitude? Could Ruben's trajectory toward learning how to be a successful student have been changed earlier in his schooling, in spite of his socioeconomic and peer network dynamics?

## Academic Support

CAMP staff and instructors were also invested in the academic well-being of the students. For example, some instructors were available outside of class to tutor (paid by CAMP) and provide additional and more individual attention to students in their math and English work. Laura attended most of the sessions, called workshops, and always seemed to take advantage of the time she had with her English instructor, William. Below is a vignette from field notes about the time I spent in one of his English tutoring workshops:

Four students are present: Maria, Cristina, Josefina, and Laura. William, their English instructor, is conducting the English workshops for a second consecutive quarter. William is helping the students with their various papers and projects in English. It is important to note that William is also the instructor of all the English courses they are taking. Although paid by the CAMP program (very minimally), he still gives his time to the students to supplement their instruction. The students are sitting at long tables working on outlines for essays, asking William a question when needed. Some questions are about the topic of their paper and whether it is appropriate for the type of paper they are writing. Others ask questions about grammar. The workshop lasts for an hour.

Luz said the planned workshops for tutoring in math were useful, because they helped her to complete her work. She was able to use the time to keep up with her coursework: "I think they're helpful. For me it was helpful, because I'm done with math. I already took the final and everything, so I'm glad. The workshop helped me to advance. I would go there for an hour and just continue my lessons. I got ahead and I finished. I have an A in that class, too. I really liked that."

Cristina remembered how useful the tutoring workshops were for her, even if she didn't have a poor grade in the class. She attended both math and English workshops. She said that they were "really useful because you know that you're going to go to that class just to work on your homework. It's helpful because you're not on your own just doing it at home, and if you have a question, the teacher is right there to help you." Cristina found that Cinthia was the most helpful of all her teachers, because of the individual attention she gave her, as well as a caring attitude. She expressed how "she always found the time to help me on my papers, and she'd always give me good ideas. She wouldn't specifically tell me to do it like this, but she'd give me ideas so I could go and redo it. She always had patience and had faith in me. I think she's the one that has helped me more in college than my other teachers."

Israel also often helped Luz with her English papers, "reading them and giving opinions." Luz's instructor from the Master Student course also remained in contact with her throughout the year, which helped her get over various obstacles, such as her confidence in writing papers: "Cinthia . . . would always tell me to do stuff, and she knows I was capable of doing some kind of assignment, and I would say 'No, I can't.' But she would pressure me towards doing it. She would encourage me to do essays that I thought I couldn't do. She's the one who has been there to help me. I'm glad to know that I have somebody there to help me out, when I'm struggling with English, my problem area."

Maria said that she felt like having supportive others in a class as a cohort was a valuable resource for her when she sought help, academic or otherwise.

> I like to be with everybody from CAMP; it helps me get to know them a lot better and who they are. Because I don't really know all of the students. But I like it, and I get a lot of help from them. If I ask them to help me with my work, they're there. They answer my questions, or whatever. Especially Cristina, she's always there with me. I think it helps me out a lot more to have them around, probably because we're in CAMP, but I like it.

Having experienced over one half of an academic year, Cristina expressed that being in a cohort with others was necessary to ensure her academic survival.

> I think I wouldn't have made it on my own without CAMP. I think I would have come to school and felt overwhelmed, because right now I have the opportunity to show my papers to you or to Lisa, and I got to meet all these people, and if I need help, they help me. We have tutoring classes. When you start college on your own, you're on your own, there are not very many people to help you. It doesn't feel like college, it just feels like school, but CAMP in general, yeah, I wouldn't make it, would have struggled a lot without CAMP.

## Schooling Knowledge and Learning of Necessity

The CAMP experience provided opportunities for the students to participate in activities that contributed to their schooling knowledge—various forms of information, knowledge, and skills that helped them navigate college. Schooling knowledge is based on the notion of having and acquiring social and cultural capital and the knowledge and way(s) of knowing to navigate social and cultural contexts and structures in society (Stanton-Salazar, 2001; Valadez, 1996). This type of schooling knowledge is often taken for granted by mainstream students, who typically come from white, middle-class backgrounds, and typically fits their ways of knowing and being (Macedo, 1994), allowing for an easier transition into everyday schooling experiences. As such, movement from marginalization through the acquisition of knowledge and skills that help students "do college" is an integral part of practice and identity.

## At CAMP Meetings

There were CAMP meetings throughout the year with the coordinator and other CAMP staff that informed the students on various topics ranging from their academic performance to issues of financial aid. Laura understood their importance and expressed that from those meetings she became "more informed about what's going on. That's important, because you have to be there, it's required. You need to have that knowledge in college so you aren't clueless."

The CAMP meetings were scheduled approximately biweekly. They were directed mostly by Lisa, the CAMP coordinator, and the students were obligated to attend. Below is an illustration of a segment of a tape-recorded CAMP meeting. This particular meeting, which takes place in the student lounge, shows Lisa helping to meet the resource needs of the students, as well as reminding students of their academic obligations and responsibilities. She informs them of the "academic workshops" (tutoring sessions) to help them improve their grades and reminds them of the academic resources available to them.

> LISA: Everybody hasn't got their disk. Make sure you get a pack of disks. You need those for the class. We have a few extra notebooks if people need to . . . the three-ring notebook. It's only one and a half inch; that's all I could get yesterday at the store, so if you need those, see me afterwards. Remember, if there's something you can't afford for class or school, see me about that, and I can try and get it for you. I can't always get it for you. Like a couple of people need a backpack—I'm not

authorized to buy everybody a backpack, but I have some that I have to donate. Sometimes people donate them and I might have a random couple of backpacks somewhere.

REYES: I have about four or five backpacks.

FEMALE STUDENT 1: I need one.

REYES: Who needs one?

FEMALE STUDENT 1: Me.

LISA: So, if you really need one or you can't afford something, let us know. Also, if people are in the upper math I have scientific calculators, but they're for checkout only. You have to give them back. They're expensive. They cost over a hundred dollars. If you check it, you're responsible for it. You have to give it back at the end of the quarter. Also, if you drop it, you break it, you buy it. Okay? So, if anybody wants to check one of those out, if you're in the upper-level math, you need a scientific one. If you're in just a lower math level and you just need, you know, a "joe blow" everyday calculator, you don't have one, let me know. And I can go to Wal-Mart and buy, like, you know, a few of them. So, let me know if you need that.

The main reason for today is I talked to a few people about this. We're going to have two workshops that are going to be required. If you're in English only, you're only required to attend the English workshop. If you're in math only, you'll only be required to attend the math workshop. If you're in both, you need to go to both workshops. They're not going to start this week or next week. They'll start the week after that, so we're giving you enough time to take the classes and go, "Okay, I've got a grasp on it. I don't need help. Okay, I'm going to need some help during the quarter." Everybody will have to go to them at first. Okay. Everybody has to go to them at first. The reason for that is because the grades last quarter. Some people didn't make the grade. They know or may not know. Remember, your requirement for CAMP—you have to maintain a 2.0 GPA. Which is cake, but obviously some people didn't make the grade. So, there's people on probation this quarter, and if you don't want to become one of them next quarter, that part will be decided at the workshop. The first workshop is going to be instructed by William. So, a lot of people already have him for English, which is cool because you can do work during the workshop that he knows about because he's your teacher. Right now the way it's going to work is they're going to be offered twice a week, two hours a week. You are only required to attend one hour. Okay. So, if you only have math, you only attend one hour of math workshop. If you only have English right now, you only attend one hour of English workshop. If you have both, you are committed to one hour of English workshop, one hour of math workshop. Okay. Starting in two weeks.

Maria said that the biweekly CAMP meetings with Lisa and others "helped me to be prepared." Because she admitted that she often forgot things, it was a good time to remind her of important dates and information about the program, or other miscellaneous information about scholarships, financial aid, or registration.

Many of the meetings, such as the one illustrated above, informed the students about what was occurring in the program and the college and how it affected them. Those who ran the meetings directed the students to various resources in the community that would help them along in their education by guiding them in how to access useful information. This practice not only provided them with information but was an opportunity to learn how to access it independently, in preparation for when they left the CAMP program. Cristina thought the CAMP meetings were helpful in her college endeavors, because "they keep you informed of all the events that are going to happen, and what's going on. Angie talks about scholarships, and now she's talking about having to do community service, so it helps a lot because you know what's going on. It helps a lot to know."

## About Financial Aid

Cristina also took advantage of the other human resources that were available for the CAMP students in two of the school advisers, Angie and Israel. They were very popular with the students because of their approachability and cultural sensitivity. Cristina remembered how they gave her individual attention in her pursuit of scholarships and financial aid, saying that "they helped me with letters of recommendation and helped me do my personal essay. Israel helped me do my personal essay, so I probably got to know them really well. And I know that I can have them as backup if I ever need them, like Israel helped me with my essay, and Angie's keeping me informed about scholarships."

Luz felt that having an adviser like Israel around was essential in preparing her for transferring to another college and in seeking out financial aid. She said, "Israel has helped me as in getting ready to go to a university. He's given me help in looking for some. I'm just happy that he's there to help me. Being by myself, I wouldn't care to look anything up. I need somebody else to help me." Israel's willingness to assist and guide her in the financial aid application process was useful in learning a key aspect of attending college for many students. Luz said she learned to have faith in her ability to seek out useful and needed information, like how to fill out the financial aid forms. She said that Israel guided her and gave her the confidence to do it on her own. She explained, "The way he tells me . . . like the financial aid. He told me I could do it on my own on the computer. I said 'No I can't, I need you.' I finally did it a week ago, and it's not hard, it's easy. I don't need his help anymore."

The CAMP students often needed guidance on how to begin the process and successfully complete financial aid and scholarship forms. Acquiring this knowledge and understanding the process was critical for many of the students, because receiving financial aid and/or scholarships was vital for their ability to continue their education. This practice led to learning a skill within their identity that reflected a source of power and skills that could be applied on a macro level of maneuverability beyond college. The skill of learning how to get financial aid is a way of accessing resources, a form of self-empowerment.

### In Learning Community Courses

Luz suggested that the Master Student segment of her Psychology/ Master Student learning community equipped her with a better sense of balancing her schedule and prioritizing. She said, "I guess the time management, when to set aside to do homework, when to tell my parents that I'm busy and can't be doing things with them because that's how they usually are with me. Yes, the time management helped."

Laura mentioned that the learning community classes helped her to be more organized, that they "showed me how to manage my time, plan everything, don't forget things. This quarter, career planning helped me, I guess, set my mind on what I want to do."

Maria felt that participating in one of the learning community courses, Computers and Career Planning, helped to guide her thinking about the requirements for studying to be a dentist. It helped her map out her goals for the next few years in her schooling.

> In career planning class, she's always telling us . . . she says a lot about our careers and stuff and what to do, and if we think we're ready for that. If not, we can change our goals. I think she's helped me a lot to understand and see whether or not I'll make it all the way, or if not, I don't have to go the whole eight years and become a dentist, because I said I wanted to become a dentist, or go half of that and maybe become an assistant or something. Depending on me. She's really helped me to decide whether I want to go all the way or only a couple years.

Many of the activities and assignments in Cristina's learning community courses provided opportunities to create a timeline for accomplishing certain things, and to set specific goals. One class in her Master Student course, she remembered, specifically focused on setting goals.

> We talked a lot about our goals. We weren't going to be like, "I want to graduate as a teacher." You had to write, "I want to transfer to UNC by the year and get a degree in teaching," and you had to be really specific. It wasn't like, "I'm going to travel to Mars in 2008." It said long-term goals, and then it had on the bottom short-term goals. One of those short-term goals I wrote was, "I want to complete my work, my career discovery worksheets in my career class, so I can receive an A in that class." And that was going to be towards my long-term goal. It also asked you what you could do specifically now and today, and a week

from today, to achieve those goals. It made you think about how you could become successful and made you write them down, and what you really wanted to accomplish, and it had to be truthful and specific.

For CAMP students like Cristina, the trajectory toward learning an identity of a successful student was going to be reached with concrete plans and creating a map to get there. As Freire (2004) implores in his approach to creating possibilities and living hope, hope must always be accompanied by tangible and attainable goals and plans to realize what is hoped for. In this learning community course, Cristina mentions how, in creating such plans, they had to be "truthful" in the expression of goals, which means they had to reflect some thought, concreteness, and specificity. Such activities were important for students like Cristina because they "made you think about how you could become successful."

## From Individuals

Luz also learned about planning for her degree, taking the appropriate coursework, and listening to advice from individuals like Israel and Lisa on the steps involved in transferring to a university.

> Basically, it was all the advice that they would give me about nursing. Because I didn't know anything. I didn't have a clue about college, what was going on. And Israel is the one who explained everything to me. Like "This is how things work" and "This is how they're going to be. If you go here to Next Step, then you can transfer to another university, but you have to maybe get the basics done before you go to a university." I didn't know any of that. They would mention them.

Maria said that having a language in common made a connection between her and her cyber mentor. She felt that it was nice to hear from someone who had already experienced college: "I think that's cool. She speaks Spanish also, so I think that's even better, because I speak Spanish too. I think it's cool, too, to talk to somebody else that you don't even know, to get ideas from them, or understand where they're coming from. They went to school and stuff like that. She gives me advice."

Ruben remembered especially how William and James not only counseled him when he was having personal and academic problems but also gave him practical and concrete ideas that might help address his struggles. He thought that James was very positive toward him, always asking him how he was doing in other classes, "even though I screwed up in his class." He was comfortable seeking them out for help.

> Both of them were, like, I don't know what it was, I felt secure in being able to ask them something. I would say, "James, I don't know what to do, and I know you're a psychology guy, so you better come up here and tell me what's up." I would go to him, "Hey, James, help me out here, man, I don't know what to do." . . . He'd actually sit down there and say, "Okay, tell me what's wrong, man." He would say, "Maybe if you tried this, maybe if you tried that. Have you ever thought about making a time sheet or try making some of these, maybe, have you even tried using your notebook?" I'm, like, "No." "Maybe that might help, Ruben!" He always gave me advice on how to be successful.

## Concluding Thoughts

In the CAMP community of practice, the CAMP students learned from instructors, counselors, peers, cyber mentors, and one another. Each student was part of an elaborate social and educational support network that provided them with information, resources, and scaffolding to help them learn how to successfully navigate college. They also received support that addressed the affective issues of learning and schooling, which helped them feel more connected and engaged with school, their coursework, and their long-term goals.

Cristina, Luz, Laura, and Maria often mentioned how they were shy and somewhat introverted. They expressed how the activities, interactions with others, and environments created allowed them to break through that shell of shyness, which helped them in many other ways. They felt that overcoming this shyness helped them to know others, to know that others in their social and academic networks were both personal and academic resources. They engaged in class more. They asked questions. And discovering and developing this aspect of their personalities had an impact on their confidence in their academic work, how they participated in class, and their abilities to engage in other ways within other social and academic networks. The women felt a great comfort in participating in these games, activities, and communities because they did not inhibit who they really could be with others.

The CAMP community of practice created additional trajectories beyond academics that helped the students to become individuals who were more comfortable with themselves and how they functioned in the college world. In this process they acquired personal tools that would help them acquire the academic tools to do well not only in the classrooms but beyond the classroom walls. This acquisition of skills, knowledge, and dispositions is part of the learning of new identities within a community of practice. The support and legitimacy given to the students by others made this teaching and learning process easier in this movement beyond their peripheral places as students from when they began (Lave and Wenger, 1991; Wenger, 1998). The students felt comfortable in this new community of practice. They felt like they were a family. The learning that occurred had an impact not only on the development of their successful student identities but also on their growing faith in others.

# 4

# Key Interactions
## as Agency
## and Empowerment

IN SCHOOLS AND CLASSROOMS, the everyday minutiae of teaching
and learning often are overlooked. The consequences of these minutiae
are rarely examined by teachers and students themselves in the frenetic
pace of everyday teaching and learning. Such minutiae are interactions
that occur on a scale that often seems inconsequential but sometimes
have important implications on teaching and learning. Cummins
(2000) calls these "micro-interactions" and suggests that such interactions are extremely powerful, especially in determining how students
perceive themselves. He suggests that it is in the space where these
micro-interactions occur between teacher and student that knowledge
is acquired and identities are negotiated and formed. For example, in
her study of high-achieving Latino students who overcame a number of social, linguistic, and/or economic obstacles in their pursuit of
academic and professional success, Gándara (1995, 1999) noted that it
was one interaction, meeting, or simple discussion with a teacher or
adult role model that prompted the students to change. That interaction encouraged the students. They felt that someone recognized their
potential. That interaction changed their life trajectory, and ultimately
how they viewed themselves in that place and time.

Building on the importance of interactions in everyday teaching
and learning, I found that there were "key interactions" that occurred

between the CAMP students and other significant players within the CAMP program—community members, CAMP staff, instructors, and peers. Key interactions are those that occurred between student and a significant individual or object and contributed a sense of agency, knowledge, or empowerment for the student. A key interaction may be the recognition of something good, or what could be good or significant, about the student and acting upon the knowledge of that potential by interacting with the student in a way that reflects that *need to recognize*. Key interactions encompass a unique blending of cultural, personal, academic, and philosophical discourse of history, present, and trajectory toward a desired possible future. They are moments when the student gains a deeper sense of self and understanding in his or her role as student in an immediate reaction to an exchange of discourse that fed that sense of self (R. Reyes, 2009).

Key interactions may originate in a brief compliment, a dialogue on the excellent improvement of academic work, an affirmation of the unique perspective and ideas that one takes to the classroom, or even a good grade with comments on an essay. A key interaction may begin with a nod of the head, a greeting in the home language of a student, or a story of experience told by an elder. Similar to what Bartlett and Holland (2002) and Holland et al. (1998) call a cultural artifact—objects that are given meaning and significance in the meeting of individuals and discourses within "figured worlds" in the creation of identities—a key interaction is ultimately defined by the stimulation of agency and the sense of potential empowerment. Cultural artifacts, when adopted, internalized, and practiced by students within their community of practice, help such students develop the ability to combat the effects of their marginalization (Bartlett and Holland, 2002; Holland et al., 1998). Similarly, key interactions can have a role in equipping marginalized students with new knowledge and insight that brings them to a new level of consciousness and awareness about their lived situations and marginalization. Key interactions are not involved relationships with students but are more cursory and implement the strategic use of additive and positive discourse and ways of being with the student that create a moment of understanding, learning, development, and ultimately empowerment. Furthermore, the impact of a key interaction may not be immediate. A key interaction may sometimes be a seed of potential impact planted within a student, and its effects may be felt and realized at any moment in the future.

Throughout the CAMP experience, the students were exposed to various contexts of learning and interactions with others—in classrooms, CAMP orientation, meetings, in individual meetings with CAMP staff or instructors, Adventure Learning courses, the student lounge. There were moments in many of these situations when students had a "key interaction" with another individual involved in the support and retention efforts of the CAMP program design. In these key interactions there was a type of "connection" of experience, history, culture, language, or community, and it provided a sense of agency or empowerment to the student. Many of the students expressed a sense of affinity with individuals from the CAMP community or with others invited to speak to them on matters of education, struggle, survival, and success. These key interactions helped to maintain the students' trajectory toward the goal of guiding/teaching/apprenticing them to be and become successful students. They brought to surface a sense of place and consciousness in their schooling continuum. Some of the key interactions that students had were not with just listening to guest speakers, but with their course instructors on matters of academics and student potential, or with CAMP staff and advisers.

## With Community Latinos: Discourse of Culture, Pride, and Resilience

Before the school year began, there was a full-day orientation for CAMP students and participants. CAMP staff and personnel made presentations on the various aspects of the program and discussed academic and other expectations. Instructors also introduced themselves, as well as the dean of the campus. There was a guest speaker, Lalo Delgado, a Chicano poet, writer, and professor, and former migrant worker, who spoke to the students about the meaning and opportunity in the CAMP experience. He was vibrant, passionate, and emotional about his own experiences in life and school, evident in his poetry readings and discussions with the students. His talk resonated with Ruben and made him think beyond his current place within the college experience:

There was one person . . . he made a speech . . . Lalo Delgado!
I remember he said something, and it just caught my eye, but
it was because of the Raiders. That year we won the Super-
bowl . . . was due to two Mexicans: the quarterback and the
wide receiver. He goes, if they can do that, we can do anything.
I really liked it, maybe we can do it, you know? Just how he put
it, he made it come out so strong. That my culture, my people,
what I am, come above all the struggles and frustrations and
make it out, and see that light, and not be stuck in the tunnel
no more.

The cultural connection that Lalo made for Ruben contributed to a
sense of knowledge of self within a grander community, the Latino
community, of struggle. Ruben found hope in the possibility of overcoming adversity because members of his community had done so,
while another prominent and passionate member gave value to this
accomplishment.

Luz, once a migrant worker herself, remembered how Lalo Delgado, who also spoke of his days of doing migrant work compared
to his life now, made her think about what a chance the scholarship
provided to get a higher education and took her back to the days of
working in the fields with her family.

When Lalo Delgado read his poems and how much he told us
about education, I realized that we have the opportunity, we
have the scholarship, so why not take advantage of it? Yes, I
really did feel that I would succeed. . . . It just reminded me
of when my sister and I would work in the fields and how
hard it was for us to have money. It was hard. We had a lot of
family problems. Now that I'm in college and look back on
it, I'm just glad that I don't have to be working in the fields
anymore. But then in a way, working in the fields made me,
not happy, but in a way proud of myself, because I did what I
was able to. I was very young. I worked for three to four years.
I really didn't care for it, I'd rather have played. But I got to
work with my sisters. It contributed to the family income. All
of us, nine of us, did the work. My six sisters, my mom and
my dad and me.

Cristina, who struggles with the English language and low self-esteem, also remembered the CAMP orientation and how Lalo Delgado made her think about pride in her heritage and the accomplishments of other Chicanos. She said, "When I see people from my heritage and culture become doctors and writers and all this, it makes me proud. I guess probably that was something that motivated me, because I heard his poems and books and how he did this and that, and that was nice."

There was also a guest speaker in the Master Student class that resonated with Luz's life and her struggles with family members that did not support her school endeavors. Although she had support from her immediate family, outside family members, who were a constant presence in her close-knit family, always questioned her pursuit of a college education. The guest speaker was a prominent Latina educator from the community who once attended Next Step Community College. Luz recalled:

> She had a speech about marriage and the way she struggled with her husband and how she got her degree eventually. She said that if you want to succeed, that it's your choice and nobody else's. Nobody else can choose for you. That really helped me, because I would always pay attention to what other people said. After the speaker said that, I realized it's my choice, and if I want to get married, I'll do so, but it's not up to them.

## From Support Staff: Understanding Struggle, Knowing Opportunity

Other key interactions happened between students and staff and instructors in the CAMP program. They were integral in creating a link of experience that would resonate with students to support their academic endeavors and provide a renewed sense of agency for them to continue on their trajectories toward being and becoming successful students in school. There were others who worked in the college, such as Israel, who played a pivotal role for CAMP students in the program and their first year of college. Israel influenced Ruben in a profound way that made him think about his culture, his lifestyle, and his role in the broader community.

He gives me advice. He comes from a similar family—his cousins—he knows what I'm going through. He lost a cousin and he knows the lifestyle. We tell stories and stuff, and he says he went through the same thing I did. He was in college and his primos [cousins] and homeboys were making fun of him going to college, like I was trying to be Mr. White Boy. But it's true, you get that. But he says, "When you've graduated, they're going to come to see you, man. Wanting help or wanting a lawyer friend or something." He says, "Don't worry about what they say, just stick to your ideals. Let their words go in one ear and out the other. They don't mean it. If you get frustrated here at school, don't blurt it out. Try to calm yourself. That's what I've done." Because, when I do get mad, it's hard to hold my temper. He'll sit down and talk to me, let me get it out, so when I go back to my next class, I'm relieved and refreshed. He keeps me motivated sometimes. He comes up to me and says, "You can do it, I don't want to see you leave." He knows what to say to certain people, like, "Come on, your raza's depending on you." I'm like, damn, why do you got to say it like that? He's right. My raza is depending on whether I make it in college. One person at a time it makes a difference. Don't think I'm racist or nothing, but when *my* people come up, it's a wonderful thing to me. If I'm one of those people who come up, maybe that's another person who sees it. That's how he makes it go, and that gives me motivation.

The Chicano ethnic identity and background was a common discourse landscape on which Ruben and Israel could communicate. Israel connected issues of education to social mobility and the notion of community and cultural representation through success in his discussion with Ruben. Such discussions also provided Ruben with a sense of agency to help him overcome his struggles inside and outside school. Because he expressed such great pride in his cultural background, the historical, cultural, and community knowledge exchanged between Ruben and Israel was a way to make strong connections between schooling efforts and a sense of place in college for a (re)developing/(re)shaping of Chicano and student identity.

Luz told me that Israel helped her on both an academic and a social level. As a Chicano who came from a similar background as Luz, he was able to relate to her in many ways, making her feel comfortable and more open.

> He gives me advice. It's the way we get along. He understands my family. He knows where we come from and how it is. When he sees me sad or something, he inquires as to why. He gives me personal advice and tells me not to waste my time dwelling on minor family problems. He says I'm going to get out of there sooner or later and not to worry about their arguments or whatever. So, I can relate to him a lot. He has a similar background. He tells me his stories from California. They wouldn't let him go out, too. Now, I guess, his sister and brother can go to Las Vegas, but he didn't have that kind of freedom with his parents. Things just change. He understands that before, with my sisters too, they wouldn't let them go out. But he says that they allow me to go out more compared to my sisters. He says that's because I'm spoiled and I'm the last sister. We get along jokingly that way.

Luz suggested that if she had not found some person who had a similar background affiliated with the college institution, it would have been a horrible year for her. She said being able to relate to someone like that allowed her to feel easier about communicating with others in the college community and staff. She said, "I think it would suck. I'd be shy still. I wouldn't talk as much." In terms of learning a successful student identity, Israel functioned as a projected potential Luz. He was able to overlap his history of experience with Luz's because, as she said, he has a "similar background," creating a narrative that she could identify with and easily understand because she was experiencing the same thing. This narrative put her at ease with the tensions of her present situation, because she knew, as he told her, she would "get out of there sooner or later."

## Through Teachers: Valuing Voice and Life in Writing

Another key interaction occurred between Ruben and his English teacher, William. Ruben talked about how William allowed him to be himself and express himself creatively based on his own background, culture, and history. In his previous schooling experiences, Ruben was always told he could not write about his gang life for writing assignments. William let him write about his gang life and told him that he was a good writer, which boosted Ruben's self-confidence. He said, "I'm really diggin' that class. [chuckle] . . . 'cause he's letting me write, where I don't have to hold back nothing. You know, I can't write about nothing I don't know." In this particular experience not only did Ruben regain a sense of confidence in his abilities as a writer, but his identity was given value in what he wrote, because what he wrote came from who he had been and who he was becoming. This interaction also renewed Ruben's faith in teachers, especially white teachers; Ruben had previously sensed that white teachers did not like Chicano students. William especially impacted Ruben's efforts with his creative writing and the work he did in William's course. Ruben said that "if he hadn't encouraged me, I don't think I would have put that much effort into it. With his encouragement, I knew I wanted that [to write well] strongly."

Ruben's reactions to William's comments and compliments on his writing were seen in the student lounge later on. Below are field notes taken from that day to illustrate this point.

I'm talking to two CAMP students, Bobby and Ruben. Bobby is at the computer working on a paper, and Ruben is standing talking to me. They have become very good friends this year. I ask them how school is going they both tell me "all right." Ruben, however, continues to tell me with growing enthusiasm that "it's cool!" because his English teacher, William, just met with him and told him that he "did a good job" on his writing assignment, which was an essay on his personal life story, and that he thought his writing "was real." Ruben has a big smile on his face, swinging his arms as if he were running a slow race, and he says, "Ain't no teacher ever told me that they thought I was doing a good job on something like my writing." He says that he thinks "it's cool" and that the teacher told him that he needed to work on his grammar a little, but the writing itself was good. Ruben then proceeds to tell me how he's been helping others with their writing class. I then see Ruben walk over to Bobby at the computer, and wanting to help him. He asks Bobby, "What are you doing, let's see," and sits down at the computer with him to read his paper. Ruben asks Bobby what he's doing his paper on and talks about ideas for the content he could put in the paper. After a few minutes of [his] helping Bobby, Ruben's mother comes in to pick him up and take him home.

Ruben exhibited a sense of pride and confidence in his writing and a new sense of ability and empowerment to help others with their writing. He felt that if an authority figure and teacher like William had enough confidence and faith in his writing abilities, then he too could begin to have those sentiments about himself, and even enact those sentiments in helping others. That key interaction between William and Ruben and its effect in how he utilized that agency was evident here in this act of support and applying his newfound knowledge and skill for others in the CAMP program.

## Concluding Thoughts

Key interactions are not epiphanies, insights, or teachable moments, although they may have some semblance to these occurrences. Key interactions are a type of teaching and learning intertwined within a moment of recognition. They are a recognition of the intertwining of history, the present condition, and possibility within a student. They bring about a new perspective, which Wenger (1998) says must be absorbed into our identities to make them a part of who we are. The absorption of these key interactions is part and parcel of learning and eventual transformation. Although key interactions most often occur between someone (or something, such as a book) who is more knowledgeable, wiser, or more experienced, they may also occur between novices. Looking at key interactions as a pedagogical and theoretical approach to teaching and learning is especially significant for marginalized student populations.

# 5

## Academic Performance and Practice

### Grades

IN PERFORMANCE AND PRACTICE of a student identity, there are also tangible results. This chapter looks at the students' grades—results of their efforts, struggles, and emerging confidence and abilities as students. In the present world of schooling we cannot ignore the fact that student performance is measured by letters and numbers. We would do the marginalized student a great disservice by minimizing the importance of grades in school. Their grades are shown here, but they are only part of the story. Because the efforts to earn grades in the CAMP community of practice go beyond the individual student, I present the experience of getting those grades from the perspectives of those who were involved in such efforts at some level. The multiple perspectives provide insight into the developing student identities from personal and academic viewpoints, and how the students presented those struggling and succeeding ways of being a student.

The story of the students' experiences to earn the grades they did presents a complicated picture of the terrain that is school, schooling, and learning to be academically successful for the marginalized student. It provides an understanding of the academic aspect of performance in the community of practice of college through CAMP and to what extent the students acknowledged and utilized the multiple forms of support throughout the academic year. Although all the students endured some level of adversity in their first college experience in earning their grades, they coped differently with it, which became a part of and defined the complexities of who and what they were becoming as students during the year.

## Laura

Laura struggled with her first English class, ENG 090–Basic Composition, and eventually had to drop it in the first quarter. She took it again in the third quarter and managed a B. She began with lower-level, developmental math courses and made good progress and excellent grades. In looking back on her first quarter in college and thinking about what a high school experience could have done for her academic performance, Laura still wished someone would have helped her to become more motivated about school, and to learn to deal with personal and academic obstacles effectively. She admitted that it took a lot of self-determination to get through the early parts of college because she had not been "pushed enough" in high school and had little guidance in dealing with academic rigor. In her first quarter of college, she suggested, "I could have been more ahead in my work, it would have been a lot easier. Instead of being frustrated, like in writing, or how to do something. It would have been easier. . . . No one pushed me enough. I wanted to be lazy a lot of times, but I had to push myself through it." Laura expressed how she persisted in her school work, despite some tendencies to shirk her school responsibilities. But what college student has not neglected their school work? For Laura, making a habit of it was not an option. She realized that she had to work through the frustrations in order to succeed. She did not want to replicate her high school experience. And she knew that she had the resources to perform better now. Although CAMP resources were available to help her in the transition to college-level work, she soon discovered that a great deal of the work was individual effort, which she exemplified in a number of ways.

Laura thought back to how she felt when she began school again through CAMP—insecure, nervous, shy, academically incapable. But after finishing one quarter with good grades and a high GPA, her attitude about her capabilities changed. Within the CAMP community of practice, Laura's identity as successful student began to evolve and move toward a more confident and capable self. Her accomplishments, along with support from friends, family, and peers and staff from the CAMP program, instilled confidence in her academic pursuits.

> I was really nervous at first, because I didn't think I could do it. Not studying for so long, being out of that mode. Sometimes I felt like giving up, because it was real stressful and I'm really a procrastinator. So it's even more stressful. I had been out of school for five years. I didn't think I would get very good grades, just thought I would pass with a C or something. Now I'm thinking more that I can do it, just keep working hard. And I have a lot of people supporting me . . . that's good.

Laura was not confident in her math and writing skills when she entered college. She had missed a lot of that academic development by not being in high school. It was, though, her fear of giving up on her academics again because of the weight of the challenges they posed for her that seemed to be ever present: "I was really afraid of my writing and math. I was okay with reading. When I got into this, I said I would not give up because that's what I used to do. And I don't want to do that, because it makes me fall back, not to try. To start something and not finish." Laura's fears in this transition from being a nonstudent to a practicing student in CAMP reflects Wenger's (1998) ideas on movement between and within boundaries of communities of practice, what he calls multimembership, and the inherent tension that arises in this process and movement. Wenger also believes that this tension is helpful in the learning process, where transformative learning may occur. Laura's hopeful and optimistic attitude toward her academic performance, even after just having practiced briefly the identity of student in CAMP, is an indication that a positive trajectory emerged from her stresses of going back to school. Part of her transformation can also be noted in her need to be persistent, her desire to not do what she frequently did in her past schooling efforts—give up. Laura's approach to her academics of "just keep working hard" coupled with the knowledge that "a lot of people" were active in "supporting" her enabled her to overcome any stress related to her schooling and study efforts. In the past, Laura was not able to overcome such schooling stresses, because she felt that she did not have the support system to enable her academic efforts. She mentioned how she "wasn't pushed by parents or teachers or anyone," which ultimately resulted in her leaving high school.

Laura felt that a great deal of being successful in college stemmed from effort and persistence. In one conversation, she mentioned how she would consistently tell herself throughout the year, "Keep your focus, not get distracted. Work hard and not give up. Keep going. Try my best." She remembered back to her first quarter in college: "It was real rough last quarter, my first time in college. I learned that I'm more confident this quarter." Laura suggested that she changed from one quarter to the next by simply overcoming her fear of schooling and her anxiety about not completing her work. But she did complete the work necessary to move on. She said, "I got past the first quarter. Now I'm here." And "here" is an important phase and level of understanding within Laura's trajectory toward the learning of a successful student identity. With access to the CAMP and college community, and the supportive individuals and networks, she was able to engage in the practice of this student identity to eventually realize her progress and position in this movement toward more learning and understanding in this process.

Laura's psychology instructor, James, noted that Laura was fairly consistent in her academic performance in his classes. He had her in his first psychology class in the first quarter (as part of the learning community), and in Psychology II, which was not a learning community. He said that she "did an adequate job. Got her work in on time. Was very consistent about being there and that didn't change from the first quarter to the last quarter," also saying that Laura would progress "just kind of going at her pace taking care of business . . . not too many ups and downs or anything like that. But it seems to be working pretty well for her." James saw Laura as a student who produced her work at a pace with which she was comfortable, while still being able to make good grades. In his perception, Laura was enacting a sense of stability and awareness in her way(s) of knowing and being that was required to maintain a student identity engaged in successful academic practice. She made progress.

Lisa, the CAMP coordinator, said that Laura "was always at school, she always left a message if she couldn't come, she hardly missed any time. She was on top of it. She didn't really have to have tutoring this go-round for English, and she wanted some. She liked William, she had a good rapport with him, and English was her toughest subject. He helped her through it, and she did it." According to Lisa's observation of her performance in school, Laura was dedicated to the requirements of the CAMP program and college. She exhibited an awareness of her strengths and weaknesses in her schooling capabilities. Laura engaged in practices, such as attending English workshops, that equipped her with the knowledge and skills to be successful in academic subjects such as writing, even though people like Lisa felt it was not necessary because she had made good progress throughout the year. This engagement exemplified Laura's awareness of the resources provided in the CAMP community of practice and how they could contribute to her developing successful student identity.

Laura's awareness and use of the multiple resources provided to her in the CAMP community of practice is illustrated in the reconstructed field notes below. English workshops were made available to students (often because of poor academic performance) at various times throughout the year to provide assistance with their writing and help them improve their grades in their English classes. Laura attended this workshop because it provided a time for her to have access to assistance that she would not otherwise have at home, and because William is also her instructor in the regular English class.

> William, the English instructor, approaches Laura and asks her what type of work she is doing, and she explains that she's planning for her essay in English 090. He acknowledges her by nodding his head and moves on to see what other students are doing. Laura tells me that she is doing a paper on a "controversial issue" and that they "have to defend our side, whether we think it is wrong or right," "have to have sources for both sides of the argument," and "had a hard time finding sources that would argue for it. . . . I sent Avon an e-mail on why they

use animal products in their makeup products." When I go to Laura during the workshop, I ask her why she attends. She tells me that it is "good for me so I can get information and more help than what I would have at home. I feel comfortable [in this workshop]. If it was someone else, I might understand what they were saying, but [with William] it's more comfortable." Laura continues to take advantage of the time in the workshop by making her plan for the paper. She shows William her final plan for her essay near the end of the session before she leaves. He acknowledges that her plan will work and that she could proceed to writing her essay.

Her efforts to improve her academic work were exemplified in her attendance at a tutoring session that she was not required to attend. Laura realized that she had to take advantage of the resources available to her if she was going to do well.

Below is Laura's transcript for the academic year. The students' GPAs are calculated according to whether they took developmental (below college-level, non–college credit) or college-level (for college credit) courses. Developmental and college-level courses are calculated separately. Developmental courses are those that are numbered at or below 090. Based on their Accuplacer computer scores, many CAMP students were placed in developmental-level courses in math and English subject courses.

Laura's feelings of success began to emerge from having successfully completed the first parts of her college experience, and then continued as the year progressed. Laura moved beyond the periphery of low self-confidence and little high school experience. This movement provided agency, confidence, and momentum in her schooling trajectory. Based on Lave and Wenger's (1991) and Wenger's (1998) notion of becoming what one is practicing in one's learning, because Laura was given the opportunity to engage in the practice of being a student, she was beginning to take on the qualities of a successful student identity. She began to express confidence and to experience academic success, as evidenced by her good grades, and instructors and staff who witnessed her progress throughout. Laura expressed an awareness of the distinction between enabling and disabling practices that contributed to her academic success, realizing that the

TABLE 5.1. Laura's Grades

| Course No. | Course Name | Credits | Grade |
|---|---|---|---|
| **Fall 2002** | | | |
| ENG 090 | Basic Composition | 5.00 | (withdrawal) |
| AAA 109 | Advanced Academic Achievement | 5.00 | A |
| PEF 122 | Team Bldg./Adventure Learning | 2.00 | A |
| PSY 101 | General Psychology I | 5.00 | B |
| Developmental-level GPA: N/A | College-level GPA: 3.58 "Dean's List" | | |
| **Winter 2003** | | | |
| MAT 030 | Fundamentals of Mathematics | 3.00 | A |
| CIS 118 | Intro to PC Applications | 5.00 | A |
| CSL 109 | Intro to Career Planning | 3.00 | A |
| PEF 112 | Physical Fitness II | 1.00 | A |
| Developmental-level GPA: 4.00 | College-level GPA: 4.00 "President's List" | | |
| **Spring 2003** | | | |
| ENG 090 | Basic Composition | 5.00 | B |
| MAT 060 | Pre-Algebra | 5.00 | A |
| PSY 102 | General Psychology II | 5.00 | B |
| Developmental-level GPA: 3.50 | College-level GPA: 3.00 | | |
| Overall Developmental GPA: 3.61 | Overall College-level GPA: 3.61 | | |

agency she enacted from her "trying hard" was more beneficial to her identity as a successful student. She said, "I think it was making me more confident and making me want to try harder for further classes or different things. I know I procrastinate a lot, but I still did it and tried hard, and I wanted to do good and be proud of myself."

Laura's sense of "trying hard" was a quality that she quickly embraced as she began to see the payoffs from such efforts in the form of good grades. With support from her family and the CAMP program, she gained confidence in her practice through her victories. Building such confidence was difficult for her to realize when she was in high school. Although Laura struggled at various intervals (first writing class) and remained peripheral with her academic writing performance at the time, she ultimately enacted positive coping strategies that led her to academic success in her other classes, and, for example, helped her overcome her fear of writing. After experiencing success and completing most of the year, Laura stated that "before, I didn't think I could do it, but now am proud of myself that I got this far." Despite her initial academic struggles, Laura's presence and efforts in this community of practice were given legitimacy by supportive others, an important part of the learning process and identity development (Lave and Wenger, 1991).

## Cristina

In a journal entry, Cristina wrote that CAMP was a special program because it "does not accept only straight-A students, but takes ordinary kids that want a chance to go to college and don't have the great grades, like myself." One of her main concerns going into college was that it would be too overwhelming for someone like her who did not have access to classes in high school that would have better prepared her. However, Cristina did well in her first year of college through CAMP. Academically, she learned to work diligently through difficult subjects. She sometimes had problems adjusting to the higher-level coursework while juggling outside responsibilities but quickly learned to plan and prioritize.

James, her psychology instructor, had Cristina for both Psychology I earlier in the year and Psychology II at the end of the year. He felt that Cristina's performance in his class was reliable. He said, "I actually think that her performance was always pretty consistent in both classes. In the first class, I felt like she held back a little bit in terms of expressing herself in doing work and kind of 'I'm just going to get this done for me.'" Although she was committed to the class and the work, he felt that she did not participate as much in class. He saw Cristina as preoccupied with her academic self-survival earlier in the year. According to James, she did what was necessary to maintain her academic performance and remain on a steady trajectory of being and doing the status quo to complete her work.

The CAMP coordinator, Lisa, saw Cristina's performance in school as one of emergence from naïveté. She saw Cristina as someone who

> really didn't know what was going to happen. She didn't know what college encompassed. High school didn't prepare her for

that, really. She was really bright, did a good job, I think they thought she was a nice girl, bright, but I don't know if they ever said, she's college material. I think the first quarter was really hard for her. English especially—it's her second language. I think she kind of breezed by it more in high school. Then when she was really challenged with writing, her writing has come along. She got an A- from William on her paper, she almost fainted. She said, "Thank God, he only gave it back to me 10 times!"

Although frustrated and intimidated earlier in the year, Cristina experienced success through trial and error in her writing. She entered the program peripheral in her knowledge of college requirements for success, but eventually learned what was required to do well in a challenging course. She endured beyond the periphery by maintaining her academic efforts, and made progress toward feeling more comfortable with her possibilities in college once she got the A-.

Cristina's academic success was exemplified by her winning academic scholarships. She performed well enough to qualify for various academic scholarships offered by the college, for which she was encouraged to apply. Below are field notes that describe a time when Cristina informs CAMP staff about her winning a scholarship.

Cristina comes in a few minutes later and sits on a black leather chair in the lounge area and says hello and asks us "What's up?" Angie, Luz, and I say hello to her, and I walk to where she was sitting and ask her about her plans for the summer so I can get an interview with her. She tells me she'll be around, so I don't have to worry. Angie then asks Cristina if she won the LAEF scholarship, and she smiles, somewhat modestly says, "Yeah. Five hundred dollars." She has a look of pride on her face, glowing, confident. We all congratulate her, smiling, telling her, "That's great!" She says, "Yeah. Now I can save some money, use that money to help pay bills, and I'm thinking about buying a computer with the scholarship money." I tell her that would be a great investment for her college career. She smiles and agrees.

This also illustrates how this financial support will help keep Cristina on her college trajectory. The scholarship represents a resource that contributes not only to her sense of agency and self-esteem, but to her material needs.

Although she initially struggled with her psychology and writing courses, she still finished the first quarter with a high GPA. She improved greatly the next quarter, even with a larger course load. As the year progressed and the courses increased in difficulty, Cristina gained more confidence in her academic abilities, especially with her writing, with which she had struggled throughout the year.

Although Cristina had to take developmental courses, they still allowed her to get to the next point in her learning and her college career. Her efforts were not futile, as they helped her to develop confidence as well as skills to use in her college-level courses. Her coping strategies with difficult courses were similar to Laura's. Rather than withdraw or give up, she put more effort into her coursework

TABLE 5.2. Cristina's Grades

| Course No. | Course Name | Credits | Grade |
|---|---|---|---|
| Fall 2002 | | | |
| ENG 060 | Writing Fundamentals | 5.00 | B |
| AAA 109 | Advanced Academic Achievement | 5.00 | A |
| PEF 122 | Team Bld./Adventure Learning | 2.00 | A |
| PSY 101 | General Psychology I | 5.00 | C |
| | Developmental-level GPA: 3.00 College-level GPA: 3.16 | | |
| Winter 2003 | | | |
| ENG 090 | Basic Composition | 5.00 | B |
| MAT 060 | Pre-Algebra | 5.00 | A |
| CIS 118 | Intro to PC Applications | 5.00 | A |
| CSL 109 | Intro to Career Planning | 3.00 | A |
| PEF 112 | Physical Fitness II | 1.00 | A |
| | Developmental-level GPA: 3.50 College-level GPA: 4.00 | | |
| Spring 2003 | | | |
| MAT 090 | Intro. Algebra | 5.00 | A |
| ENG 121 | English Composition I | 5.00 | B |
| PSY 102 | General Psychology II | 5.00 | A |
| | Developmental-level GPA: 4.0 College-level GPA: 3.50 | | |
| | Overall Developmental GPA: 3.50 Overall College-level GPA: 3.52 | | |

and earned high grades. When discussing her academic performance, Cristina said, "To me right now, I just feel successful, because I'm keeping my good grades. But to be completely successful to me would mean being very dedicated to my work. I've been successful so far because I took this opportunity seriously." As part of Cristina's developing successful student identity, she formed strategies that resonated in her persistence and resilience. Confidence in her own abilities was one of those strategies and anchored her present efforts and future plans for continued academic success.

## Luz

Academically, Luz performed well throughout the year. She was confident in her abilities to do the coursework but did not open up to others easily. She still struggled with the role of romance in her life and its potential impact on her educational pursuits. But she seemed to be learning how to deal with these tensions effectively. The only academic problems that arose came about when she had to leave with her family to Mexico near the end of the last quarter of the CAMP program and academic year. She did successfully complete those courses upon her return.

The psychology instructor, James, found that Luz exhibited characteristics in her performance throughout the year that showed growth and courage. He said that at the end of the year, he saw her as

> much more independent there and thinking on her own, responding on her own. Taking risks. It was a real striking moment in the class where she had to do a reaction paper. And she could have done it on anything. And she chose to do it on something very personal, and she chose to share that to the whole class and this was a mixed class. It wasn't just CAMPers and it was fairly early in the quarter. So, in my opinion that was a big risk. It showed that she was comfortable with herself and saying, "This is how I want to use this environment." So, I was really impressed with that. And she was doing excellent work at the time she had to leave. She came to me. She told me about her situation. She made arrangements in terms of taking care

of her coursework. All very independent, which shows a lot of commitment on her part.

He felt that Luz was exhibiting characteristics of a responsible student and remaining committed to what was needed to do well in class (even when she had to leave to Mexico with her family). According to James, Luz was steadily maintaining what was already visible as a strong student identity. She was not exhibiting any negative consequences of her internal confusion about romance and the pressures from her extended family, seemingly maintaining a trajectory in being a successful student while acknowledging the other personal and family trajectory.

Lisa felt Luz was reliable and tenacious in her schooling efforts. She illustrates a time that Luz was struggling with an English class, because she did not like how the instructor taught the class, but remained committed. Luz finished the course with a B-, and considering what Luz thought was the lack of high-quality instruction and guidance, Lisa thought that "she did really well. She's a really good girl. You call and ask her to be there, she's there, on time, she doesn't miss things. She doesn't come up with excuses all the time. She just shows up." Luz sometimes struggled with various aspects of college, such as bad instructors. But, as Lisa explains, Luz was a reliable student. She was committed to her work. This willingness to endure this type of struggle and adversity exemplifies the strength in her student identity and desire to remain on her trajectory toward her goal of becoming a nurse.

Another example of Luz's desire to succeed and her strong student identity was when she had to withdraw from the last academic quarter to go to Mexico for a family emergency. Below are field notes that illustrate a time I spoke with her on the phone and expressed my concern for her grades, because she had put forth so much effort to earn them.

> Lisa tells me that Luz is going to Mexico for a family emergency. I call Luz and she confirms that she and her family are leaving for Mexico in a few days for an unspecified family emergency. I tell her I'm concerned that it will affect her grades because she was making all As in her classes, but she tells me that

she's taking incompletes and will make up the work when she gets back. I tell her that it is difficult to make up incompletes, but she assures me that she will get it done. She promises she will return in June, but is not sure exactly when. I hang up the phone and am a bit worried for her because she seemed a bit dismayed that she had to leave school. She's a hard worker, though, and I'm sure she will finish the incompletes. She likes to get good grades.

Luz returned from Mexico early in the summer after the academic year and fulfilled her incompletes successfully. Although briefly taken off her trajectory toward her school goals, she was resilient and determined enough to recover and continue.

TABLE 5.3. Luz's Grades

| Course No. | Course Name | Credits | Grade |
|---|---|---|---|
| Fall 2002 | | | |
| ENG 060 | Writing Fundamentals | 5.00 | A |
| AAA 109 | Advanced Academic Achievement | 5.00 | A |
| PEF 122 | Team Bldg/Adventure Learning | 2.00 | A |
| PSY 101 | General Psychology I | 5.00 | B |
| Developmental GPA: 4.00    College-level GPA: 3.58 "Dean's List" | | | |
| Winter 2003 | | | |
| ENG 090 | Basic Composition | 5.00 | B |
| MAT 080 | Math & Basic Algebra | 3.00 | A |
| CIS 118 | Intro to PC Applications | 5.00 | A |
| CSL 109 | Intro to Career Planning | 3.00 | A |
| PEF 112 | Physical Fitness II | 1.00 | A |
| Developmental-level GPA: 3.50    College-level GPA: 4.00 "Dean's List" | | | |
| Spring 2003 | | | |
| MAT 090 | Intro. Algebra | 5.00 | *A |
| ENG 121 | English Composition I | 5.00 | *A |
| PSY 102 | General Psychology II | 5.00 | *B |
| Developmental-level GPA: 4.00    College-level GPA: 3.50 "Dean's List" | | | |
| Overall Developmental-level GPA: 3.72    Overall College-level GPA: 3.68 | | | |

*NOTE: Since Luz had to withdraw early from the spring quarter for personal reasons and go to Mexico with her family, she was initially given "incompletes" after arrangements were made with her instructors. She fulfilled the requirements for the incompletes and received the grades shown.

Luz was strong academically and had a propensity for overcoming adversity, which is why she performed so well in her first year of college through the CAMP program. She was always present in class (except when she had to go to Mexico for the family emergency), as well as the activities. She struggled at times with the competing discourses of her ambitions and the fears of romance and domesticity anchored in unsupportive distant family. Luz was, indeed, learning and taking on the characteristics of a successful student identity.

## Maria

Maria started college in the second quarter of the CAMP program and the academic year. She was transitioning from having taken some GED courses there at the college but had not taken college-level courses until she entered CAMP. She struggled with math and English but still made average and above-average grades in those courses the first quarter. The second quarter shows the results of her struggles—personally and academically.

Tina, the computer instructor, felt that Maria initially was unsure of her capabilities as a student. She talked about how she observed great progress in not only Maria's work but also her sense of self as a student.

> Maria at first really felt intimidated. She was kind of wondering, "Can I do this?" She was a little low on self-concept. And I think that her work was okay, but the more positive feedback I gave her, the better her work got. And her last project was very well done. So I think she developed a lot over the quarter, and a lot of that was just positive reinforcement. Because she was capable, just really lacking the self-confidence to say, "I guess I can do this. I understand and I can do it." And to balance that with her family life, I think she did a very good job. But she definitely came in intimidated and a little low in self-confidence.

Maria was becoming empowered as a student throughout the course as she was engaging more and receiving positive feedback from Tina. This experience reflects how Maria had a low self-perception as a capable student, keeping her peripherally motivated until she was apprenticed and assisted beyond her marginal existence by a more knowledgeable other who encouraged and supported her.

Lisa noticed about Maria that "she was happy to be at school and was surprised at how well she did. She got a 4.0 that first quarter, she got all As. She was really proud of herself." As the year progressed and Maria began the spring quarter, Lisa noticed that her responsibilities at home with her children were starting to become overwhelming as her coursework increased in difficulty. Lisa noted, "It started getting harder and harder to find people to watch them. She just got behind, and then she finally just came and said, 'I don't know what to do.'" Her mother was initially watching her children but got a full-time job near the end of the academic year two weeks before Maria was to complete the quarter. Lisa acknowledged that Maria's outside responsibilities were a lot for her to handle while she was in school. She had the desire and agency, but her life situation made it complicated to be a successful student.

Not even CAMP, through all of its programmatic efforts and design, could ameliorate this situation. The college and CAMP community of practice and support was not adequate in helping Maria deal with the overlap of her schooling and life trajectories, which impacted how she dealt with her identities as both student and mother. It was a clash of identities, grounded in the reality of socioeconomics and the social realities of the hardships of teen motherhood. Below is a short vignette of field notes of the time she told me of the news.

It is the end-of-the-year CAMP Bar B Q, a couple of weeks before the end of the quarter and the end of the CAMP program for the year. I see Maria in the lounge, sitting on a leather couch that the students had often used, and ask her how she's doing and she says "not so good." She tells me that she's not sure if she'll finish the year because she needs to stay at home with her two sons because she has no one at this time to take care of them, like she did earlier in the year. She almost seems embarrassed, ashamed that it has come to this. She appears sad and has a look of disappointment in her eyes, but still with some hope, because Maria always expressed a desire to do well in school.

Maria did leave the program a few days later.

As her transcript indicates, Maria had to withdraw from all of her courses in the spring quarter because of personal and family issues. Her first quarter in the CAMP program, she earned a 4.0 GPA in her college-level courses, which are calculated separately from developmental courses. The 4.0 Maria earned had a great impact on her self-confidence and the possibilities open to her because she experienced success. She excitedly expressed, "It made me think that I could do it. I shouldn't stop myself. . . . But now that I've experienced it, I know that I can. I know that I can keep going." Maria moved toward a new awareness of not only her academic abilities but her persistence. Her ability to engage in the practice was pivotal in her learning and developing a successful student identity.

## Ruben

In beginning his college work, Ruben felt confident about his abilities to handle college-level academic work. It was his discipline and study habits that impeded his progress in classes. He consistently procrastinated, not being able to balance personal and social issues

TABLE 5.4. Maria's Grades

| Course No. | Course Name | Credits | Grade |
|---|---|---|---|
| Winter 2003 | | | |
| ENG 060 | Writing Fundamentals | 5.00 | C |
| MAT 030 | Fundamentals of Math | 3.00 | B |
| CIS 118 | Intro. to PC Applications | 5.00 | A |
| CSL 109 | Intro. to Career Planning | 3.00 | A |
| PEF 112 | Physical Fitness II | 1.00 | A |
| Developmental GPA: 2.75 | College-level GPA: 4.00 "President's List" | | |
| Spring 2003 | | | |
| ENG 090 | Basic Composition | 5.00 | *AW |
| MAT 060 | Pre-Algebra | 5.00 | *AW |
| PSY 102 | General Psychology II | 5.00 | *AW |
| Developmental GPA: N/A | College-level GPA: N/A | | |
| Overall Developmental GPA: 2.75 | Overall College-level GPA: 4.00 | | |

*NOTE: AW indicates that student withdrew from the course.

with his school work. His inability to handle multiple tasks and realize the need to adapt practices that would allow him to be and become successful was evident in his handling of coursework.

James noted that Ruben had certain good student qualities, such as his class participation. But he felt that Ruben's complex life did not allow him to manage the course requirements effectively and successfully.

> He would participate extensively in the oral aspects of the class. He'd be in class and he'd listen and he'd have comments and he'd have questions and things like that almost every class period. Some of which were quite insightful, and showed that he had some grasp of the concept that we were talking about. But then in terms of turning in any formal assignments, it just did not happen. In both quarters, he came to me outside of class and talked about some personal issues and challenges that had come, and so my generalization from that that's kind of his life style. That he has these crises that come up in his life on a fairly regular basis. And whether it's his resources or whether it's his coping strategies, they really take a lot out of him in terms of "I got to manage this. I've got to get on top of this stuff right here, right now." And then everything else, including college, just takes a back seat. I can't speak to whether that was an accurate assessment on his part or it was an excuse on his part. I don't know about that, but it was interesting to see that the same type of process emerged in both quarters.

Because Ruben would mismanage his academic commitments so often, James was unsure whether his reality was just too complicated to work with college life. Ruben's performance as a student in James's class remained peripheral in terms of fulfilling that which is required to be a successful student, such as turning in work. His social participation in class did illustrate ways in which he attempted to make progress toward learning to be a successful student. But this was only one aspect of many in this identity. The other qualities required to be a successful student could not be manifested for Ruben.

Lisa knew Ruben's struggles very well. She knew that he was dealing with financial and other responsibility issues at home, while trying to learn what is required to be a successful student. Lisa talked about the following pertaining to Ruben.

> He wasn't in a gang here, but he still had friends that were. They would call him and he would get involved, and it was hard for him to say no to a lot of the stuff. He would go when they would call him. Even though he had a stack of homework, that brotherhood would call, and he would go. And then he would come the next day and say, "I didn't finish anything. I went and did this," or "This happened." And he took a lot of risks. He was aware of them but just didn't have the maturity to say no yet. He did, toward the end, some things, but he just dropped way behind. I don't think he realized the intensity of it or how serious you have to be.

Ruben's outside influences were still too powerful in his life. They did not reconcile well with his trajectory and efforts (or lack thereof) in school. He wavered between obligations toward school and peers, often choosing peers first. He was at times successful, but not enough to warrant successful academic/student performance or progress. His participation in the CAMP and college community of practice did not influence him to the degree that it did other students, as evidenced by his struggling sense of self between borders of communities of school and outside life.

Class participation was the extent of Ruben's engagement in academic work. He rarely turned in written work, and when he did, it was typically late. His participation in the college and CAMP community of practice remained peripheral at the academic level. Socially, he evolved and immersed himself more in the various activities of class and CAMP. His vocal involvement and physical presence were symbolic of his advancement beyond the periphery of his schooling existence by at least becoming more involved in schooling than he had in the past. But that was only in partial fulfillment of being and becoming a successful student. The social and personal participation were stages of his beginning development toward a successful student identity, while the academic aspects of studying and producing work remained difficult to manage for Ruben.

Ruben began the year with mediocre-to-low grades but was at least able to complete the courses. As the year progressed, he began to resort to withdrawing from courses or getting an "incomplete" to finish the course later (which he did not do). The last quarter of the year shows that he withdrew from all the courses and, according to CAMP, was not able to successfully complete the year with a 2.0 GPA, as required by the CAMP contract.

Ruben struggled with school for numerous reasons—family obligations, peer pressure, inability to balance commitments, and a lack of schooling experience that socialized him to know how to succeed academically. His early grades reflect that he put forth little effort in his core courses, but the second quarter shows he regained confidence, which translated into improved work, attendance, and ultimately better grades. Again, though, he withdrew from and did not complete two core content courses. The last quarter indicates

TABLE 5.5. Ruben's Grades

| Course No. | Course Name | Credits | Grade |
|------------|-------------|---------|-------|
| Fall 2002 | | | |
| ENG 060 | Writing Fundamentals | 5.00 | C |
| AAA 109 | Advanced Academic Achievement | 5.00 | F |
| PEF 122 | Team Bldg/Adventure Learning | 2.00 | A |
| PSY 101 | General Psychology I | 5.00 | F |
| | Developmental-level GPA: 2.0    College-level GPA: .67 | | |
| Winter 2003 | | | |
| ENG 090 | Basic Composition | 5.00 | AW* |
| MAT 060 | Pre-Algebra | 5.00 | I** |
| CIS 118 | Intro to PC Applications | 5.00 | C |
| CSL 109 | Intro to Career Planning | 3.00 | C |
| PEF 112 | Physical Fitness II | 1.00 | A |
| | Developmental-level GPA: (incomplete)    College-level GPA: 2.22 | | |
| Spring 2003 | | | |
| ENG 090 | Basic Composition | 5.00 | AW* |
| MAT 080 | Math & Basic Algebra | 3.00 | AW* |
| PSY 102 | General Psychology II | 5.00 | AW* |
| | Developmental-level GPA: N/A    College-level GPA: N/A | | |
| | Overall Developmental GPA: 2.0    Overall College-level GPA: 1.33 | | |

*NOTE: AW indicates that student withdrew from the course.

**NOTE: I indicates that work for the course was "incomplete."

that the numerous pressures and responsibilities in his life took a toll on his efforts in school. He said he enjoyed the idea of college and what it could do for him but also admitted, "I don't recommend it if somebody's having struggles. You got to come here with a clear, level head before you can even enter here. Because if you don't, and you don't get shit straightened out in your life, you're going to be struggling, like me."

Although Ruben did not complete the requirements for the last quarter's courses, he symbolically "completed" the academic year by continuing to attend CAMP activities, such as the end-of-the-year CAMP Family Bar-B-Q, and receiving recognition for having participated in the CAMP program. He was happy to receive this recognition.

## Concluding Thoughts on the Students' Grades

There were a number of similarities between the five student case studies and their academic experiences and how they dealt with the challenges of college coursework, but three prominent themes emerged in their pursuit of good grades: (1) they all took remedial math and reading courses, (2) they all had personal and life issues that often impeded their academic progress but sometimes used such hurdles to fuel desire and contribute to their resiliency, and (3) the students persisted.

Laura faced her struggles and fear through diligence. She struggled with writing but adopted and used the resources available—her teachers, CAMP tutors, CAMP staff—to help scaffold her writing. Although she initially took a number of developmental courses that were not for college credit, they were necessary in her learning and development because they were appropriate for her academic abilities at the time. Laura's leaving high school in the ninth grade created an academic and schooling gap for her that had to be filled with the developmental courses. Experiencing success contributed to her trajectory of learning how to be more successful.

Similar to Laura, Cristina struggled with her writing and math. But, like Laura, she persisted in her efforts, which paid off in improved quality in her work and, ultimately, her good grades on writing assignments. Language was also a struggle for her. Cristina may have been on the academic track she was on in high school because English is her second language. As such, she knew that her high school coursework did not prepare her for college-level coursework. She gained more confidence as she was experiencing success and even won an academic scholarship, which was an immediate, tangible reward for her efforts. Although she did not participate much in class, she was still productive in her coursework. This created a beneficial cycle of effort/persistence and earning/maintaining good grades. Cristina entered college unsure of her academic and linguistic capabilities, but confidence was a core aspect of her successful student identity process and development. Cristina's confidence anchored her movement from her marginal place in academics and schooling toward her new understandings of what was required to do well in school.

Luz was academically strong, but she struggled with tensions between the discourse of romance, relationships, and domesticity and those of her own desires to be in college and pursue a career. Coming from a migrant family, she knew struggles well. Perhaps that is what provided strength and motivation to do well in school. Like Cristina and Laura, Luz was also very resilient and dealt with adversity well in her first year of college, which was reflected in her good grades. Her ability to withdraw from school to deal with a family situation in Mexico and then return to school to successfully complete her courses showed her determination. Her high GPA shows that she was academically strong and ready to take on increasingly difficult college coursework. Like Laura and Cristina, Luz also had to take developmental courses, for which she did not get college credit. She struggled with math and English courses but completed them with good grades.

Maria had the desire to be in college, do well, and improve her life situation so that she could provide more to her children. But, in this case, desire was not enough. Her situation as a single mother, with two young children who were not yet school age, weighed heavily in her personal, social, and academic decisions and efforts. As a result, many of her grades suffered as the year progressed. Although the CAMP program is designed to address some issues of socioeconomics (by providing the scholarship) and academics (through tutoring and a strong academic network of support), Maria's case reflects how some student realities are too difficult and complex in the pursuit of providing access and opportunity.

As described by one of her instructors, Maria was also very shy and quiet and seemed to lack confidence in her academic abilities. She did well in her developmental courses but struggled when she reached college-level coursework. It should be noted that the time that she was taking college-level courses coincided with when she began to struggle with finding help with her children while she attended school. As such, it may not have been the academic difficulty with coursework as much as the issues with time and space in her life that complicated committing to the rigors of school in the way that she wanted.

Ruben felt that people who have life issues cannot deal with going to college at the same time. But he may have needed help in learning how to handle life while learning how to learn, how to commit to academic pursuits in college and effectively manage those commitments. Everyone knew of his struggles, and of his past. But his past was and will always be a part of Ruben—whether in school or not. Ruben exhibited glimpses of doing well academically, which reveals that he is capable of doing the work. One instructor talked about how he vocally expressed his conceptual understandings in class, but such understandings seemed to stop there and could not be seen in the scant written work that was turned in.

In regard to the students' grades and what they did to earn them, there were tensions, and sometimes contradictions, between students' desire to succeed and do well as students and the actual ability to enact that desire. Much of this stemmed from their history of marginalization. Laura, Cristina, and Luz managed these tensions well. But Ruben's and Maria's efforts in coursework, influenced by the complexities of their outside lives and obligations, created a wavering, and often receding, effect in their trajectory from peripheral positions in their schooling toward being and becoming successful students. Wenger (1998) acknowledges that in that space and transition from one community of practice to another, there are risks, and in those risks there is the inherent possibility of failing to practice like other members of the community. As a result, according to CAMP program expectations for academic performance, Ruben and Maria did not succeed in producing college-level academic work adequate to warrant progress and success at various times throughout the year. They both acknowledged their shortcomings in school but expressed how the experience in college gave them insight into what was required to do well, as well as what *not* to do in order to succeed. But they also felt that they succeeded in other ways. So other ways of learning did occur for them, beyond what their grades showed. Indeed, all students learned a great deal from their unique experiences and circumstances.

# 6

# Emerging and Evolving Identities as Successful Students

THE CAMP STUDENTS changed and continued to change. But in what ways? I interviewed each student at approximately the same time throughout the academic year, and then one last time four or five months after the end of the CAMP program year. In each interview there was always a hint of change in their voices, their use of words, and their demeanors. Their words—their stories of experiences in learning and change—seemed to be evolving and accumulating new understandings as they continued on their student trajectory at different moments, after certain events, throughout the year. Their changes began in their key interactions with guest speakers, in the learning community courses, in Adventure Learning, the day they received the CAMP scholarship. Their changes began in struggles and success. Their changes began in getting good grades and bad. And with these changes came changing identities.

Since identities are not merely an internalization of an understanding of the self-concept but are also a projection of oneself (Holland et al., 1998), this chapter provides the observations and perspectives of those who were also privy to the change and development they saw in the students—Lisa (CAMP coordinator) and three instructors, James (psychology instructor), William (English instructor), and Jane (math instructor). Along with my own analysis of what the students said and did based on interviews and field notes, the other perspectives provide a triangulation of data to present whether, indeed, the students projected any sense of evolving or emerging identities as successful students.

## Laura: "I feel like I can do anything"

After having had Laura earlier in the year in his English class, then in a later class, an English instructor, William, noticed quite a change in her personality and the overall way she presented herself. He noted that a change in her confidence was needed for her to feel more comfortable and confident, so that she could successfully navigate college work and culture.

> She's a changed person. She finishes a sentence. She sits up and speaks in a perfectly normal voice without hesitation; she has become more comfortable being here, being in college, and probably being in an English class too. It's a major transformation that I've seen with her. Obviously, this term has just started, so I don't know what her work is going to be like. But just the personality that she brings to the classroom, it's a whole transformation, she's a different person. And that's something that needed to happen. She probably realized that first of all she needs to be able to stand up and be herself in order to survive here, but also I think she's realized that this isn't such a scary place after all, and she's become more used to it and aware of what it can do for her. It's somewhat speculation, obviously, but the transformation just that I can see in her is amazing.

From William's perspective, Laura went through a dramatic change during the year. She presented a new sense of self that was reflected in her participation in the classroom. This aspect of her personality now was an integral part of her ways of engaging in and communicating with the outside world, including school. William felt that Laura learned to adopt a new sensibility of self and way of being as a student in order to maintain her trajectory in being and becoming an identity of a student working hard and trying to succeed.

Lisa noted, "When she first came, you couldn't even hear her talk in the interview. We'd ask her a question, she would answer, and it was so low and she'd barely open her mouth so that you could barely understand her. Then, to have her come in my office and make a joke, or stand there and laugh with the other kids, that's incredible . . . for her to ask for help and say, What do I need to do for this, etc." Building on what William saw in Laura, Lisa also saw her transformation of personality and ways of expressing herself. Lisa saw significant change in how Laura participated in the CAMP program and college community, exhibiting more confidence in her ability to dialogue and interact with others.

From Lisa's perspective, Laura seemed to be a more empowered and enabled student, illustrating a move from a peripherally situated place as a withdrawn student toward someone more confident. Lisa stated, "She already registered for fall. She's on top of it now. She's not this little shy, step-on-me . . . she's a tough person and has grown a lot. So I think getting that self-confidence is very evident in that girl. You can really tell that she's grown a lot personally. She has self-confidence, she talks, you can understand her and hear her now. She drives around and has friends."

Lisa also observed that Laura gained confidence in her ability to navigate some of the aspects college students must deal with outside of class while attending college. My field notes below illustrate this point.

> Lisa tells me that she saw Laura yesterday go to the school by herself. She drove by herself, with no boyfriend or parent by her side, and registered, bought her own books, and did everything on her own. This is quite a contrast from last year, when Laura could barely speak loud enough to tell us her name, and was very shy about doing things on her own. Lisa expresses how she feels that Laura is a success story because of how independent she felt Laura appeared when seeing her do those things on her own and realizing that no CAMP staff or personnel were there to take those steps to continue her education. Laura is apparently learning to make her way in college.

According to Lisa's observation, Laura was enacting qualities of independence and empowerment to make her way through college in continuing her trajectory as college student. Laura was enabled to function within the larger college community of practice without the scaffold of CAMP and the support and social network.

Laura thought about being a successful student in terms of stages. She felt she needed to identify first with simply "working hard," then taking on notions and identities of success as she met goals and completed her work. She said, "I think it's starting 'cause as a college student right now I guess I see myself as working hard, I guess that's my identity . . . as a hard worker. And, and I guess . . . just maybe figuring it out." For Laura, what rooted her and her hard work was having a vision of what was required to be successful. As she explains here, she needs to continue "being a student . . . now trying to see my future or see my goals."

Laura said, "I think I've changed a lot. In the beginning, I was really quiet, but now, I'll talk a bit more, more openly, not much, but I'm getting there. I can be more confident in myself. If I get stressed out, I can handle it better." Although still quiet and soft-spoken in her conversations, Laura indeed seemed more confident and optimistic. She commented that being in the CAMP program was helping her see a possible and real future. She said that this was a place and a time that was positively contributing to her trajectory toward her goals. She found herself open to new opportunities, ones "that will help me in the future. Well, this opportunity. It will help me because when I graduate, I'll be able to get better jobs and pursue what I want to do. No one telling me I'm not successful."

This process included engaging in the work required to get to the next step of her education, recognizing that her identity as a successful student will take on its own shape and process as she continues. She said, "I need to, you know, it'll be, you know, to figure it out. It'll progress, I guess, as I go on." She told me that she felt this identity as a good and positive student emerged from beneath layers of her past, with the present experience helping it to come about. She said in regard to her identity as student, "I think it before was, like, like hidden, I think. But now that, that I've gone through this and I've seen that, that I can, by doing hard work and you know just sticking to it, I can do it." Laura here indicates that it was the act of practice itself that helped reveal a new and possible self of her identity as student. But although this aspect of identity was "hidden," it was always there. It was just waiting for an event, interaction, or experience to help it emerge in the learning of a new identity.

When asked if she had changed after one year of attending college through the CAMP program, she stated: "I became more confident about schoolwork and outside of school. I spoke up more. I don't know. It just makes me feel confident to try to succeed in school and in the world. I can do a lot more, learn a lot more. It's helped me to learn more about the world and about life and school. I feel like I can do anything."

## Concluding Thoughts on Laura's Change

Laura had issues of low self-esteem and confidence that began in middle school and transferred to high school, which played a role in her academic struggles. She was constantly on the periphery of her learning and participation in the larger social and schooling world. In her early high school years, she did not have many opportunities to engage in positive and collaborative communities of practice, in and outside of classrooms. She mentioned that she felt her teachers did not care, similar to the feelings of the Mexican youth in Valenzuela's (1999) study on "subtractive schooling," which contributed to the students, as well as the teachers, giving up on the possibility of a collaborative learning environment. Laura too felt like she had no choice but to give up in high school by leaving it entirely.

Earning her GED and then winning the CAMP scholarship functioned as an entry point into a community of practice that provided a space for engagement and the practice of being a student again. Her participation in the program began peripherally, because she was deeply entrenched by her low self-perception as a student influenced by negative experiences with individuals, in and out of school, before entering the program. The design of the CAMP program emphasized learning in a community through its cohort philosophy in classes and other activities. This allowed Laura to consistently socialize with others and present herself vocally, physically, and academically within a safe environment. She was personally and academically developing various sides to her new identity as a college student, contributing to her agency through successful completion of projects, courses, academic quarters, and, finally, the academic year. As she was being successful in her college course-work, she "started seeing how good I was doing in my work, try-ing to reach my goals, or see myself reach my goals," suggesting a notion of forward trajectory, toward a future, and the next point in her learning and development.

Laura also rarely felt alone in the process and practice of being a student again, as she was constantly surrounded by accessible people and resources who she knew would accept her as she was, a stark difference from what she felt in high school. She said that "it helped too that a lot of people and a lot of the other students, you know, would talk to you or weren't afraid to, you know, to help you out if you need help. Everybody is, like, really nice. So that helped too." She also noted the different "assisters" throughout her first year in college, providing comfort, insight, or advice and information about what it took to be successful in classes and coursework. Everybody was helpful to her, but one of her learning community instructors was integral in the development of her courage, self-esteem, and voice. The instructor empathized with Laura's fear of having to pres-ent in front of a class as well as provided suggestions on her prepara-tion. Reflecting the apprenticeship aspect of teaching and learning in a community of practice (Lave and Wenger, 1991), the instructor apprenticed Laura in the ways of being a successful student by giving her tips from her own practice of speaking in front of others, along with academic skills such as writing.

Laura's act of being a student within this community of practice provided an opportunity for her to "test herself" and the possibil-ity of being a successful student. She did not know until she tried and achieved whether she could be successful in college, helping to move her beyond the periphery of learning. Much of her movement was propelled by the use of her voice—both actual and symbolic—in dialogue with others, participation in class, and articulating her ideas and learning in more resounding ways than she had done in the past. She suggested that since she "spoke up more" she began to "feel con-fident" that she could "do a lot more, learn a lot more." Laura's voice, "as it relates to the variety of ways by which students actively partici-pate in dialogue and attempt to make themselves heard and under-stood" (Darder, 1991, p. 66), was now a tool for empowerment. The use of her voice helped her to better understand the world and to understand her capabilities.

Laura was not sure she would succeed in college, because she had not been in school for so long. She did not have a sense of a successful or positive student identity until she engaged in the actual practice of "doing college" within a community of others who were on the same trajectory and who could scaffold her efforts and accomplishments. The apprenticeship provided by CAMP staff, instructors, peers, and her family support system provided personal and academic knowledge and agency that contributed to the knowing of her self as a student and helped shape her identity of a hard worker in school.

## Cristina: "Now I see myself like I could accomplish anything"

James, psychology instructor, and also an integral part of the CAMP learning communities curriculum, who team-taught with Cinthia, initially saw Cristina as lacking in self-confidence but saw tremendous change at the end of the year, when he had her in his second psychology class. He said, "I felt like she was more confident in herself towards the end. It's like 'I can do this. I don't have a problem with this.'" He thought she was more relaxed about doing school work and exhibited confidence in her abilities, suggesting that she expressed a way of being that said that "she doesn't have to pay attention to every single detail and she'll still do quite well." According to James, Cristina presented a way of being a student that allowed her to understand and assess, but not get bogged down with, the details of school and daily situations in an effective way. She took on characteristics of a student who learned how to navigate college and its requirements, shown through her confidence and ability to continue to get good grades.

Lisa thought Cristina learned the intricacies of making her way through college, and how it would require time and life management skills at a level that affected every aspect of her life:

> I think Cristina thought she could work full-time, and that was
> a realization that came right away. We said, "We don't let you

do that." So she had to cut back hours. That was hard at home, because she was a major contributor to the family income, but her mom let her do it because she knew school was a priority. And Cristina learned how to adjust, and she realized how much of a time commitment college was. I don't think she was really thinking it was going to be that much time. She's grown so much and taken on responsibilities.

Cristina was seen here as a student who quickly realized the need to prioritize and balance life commitments. Although needing to reduce her work hours to meet her academic obligations with CAMP, it was important to Cristina's mother for her daughter to do well in school. She presented a student identity that showed growth and maturation in managing the trajectories in which she was engaged—at home and at school.

Cristina recalls, "When I started college, at the beginning I was really scared I wasn't going to make it. I didn't have that courage." This changed as she looked back on the year, her successes and failures, but most notably the fact that she made good grades and completed her first year of college. She said, "And now I feel like, I know I'm going to become successful. Before, I was just scared and uncertain. Really scared." Her eventual confidence came from accomplishment and having had the opportunity to engage in practices that allowed her to have opportunities to struggle, learn, and become.

In high school and early in the CAMP program,, Cristina didn't see herself as a successful or potentially good and successful student. Because of her hard work and dedication to her schooling, she eventually saw herself differently and in a positive light.

Before, I didn't feel like I was very much [a good student]. Now, I feel so proud of myself. Now I feel like I am so much, and can become so much. I don't know, all this college stuff is very important to me. It's changing my way of seeing myself. Now I see myself like I could accomplish anything, and I could do it. Before, I had good grades but for basic courses. I never took college classes and stuff in school, so I see myself differently. Before, I knew I had pretty good grades in school, so I just felt happy for myself. But now I feel so great, like I'm really accomplishing a lot. I feel proud of myself. I think that I have worked very hard in college for everything, so I see myself very differently. I see I've accomplished so much for myself.

Although Cristina exhibited great confidence and growth in her development as a college student, one interaction I had with her made me realize that marginalized identities who have been doubtful of their abilities will always have lingering feelings and doubts.

I'm speaking with Cristina about scheduling an interview with her, and she begins to talk about her past year in college and tells me, "I don't know if I'm gonna make it. Do you think I'm gonna make it in my next years in college?" She seems nervous about her future college years and tells me she is particularly concerned about the upper-level courses she's going to take, and whether she'll be able to pass them and be successful. Ultimately, I reassure her that she will do just fine. That if she made it this far, she can go even further. Cristina is in transition at this point, preparing to move on to the second year of her college career and about to be out of the CAMP program. I believe she just wants someone to give her their vote of confidence in her abilities as a student.

Here, Cristina displays doubts about her capabilities in handling future college experiences and challenges. We all experience lingering doubts about our abilities—as a scholar, as an educator, as a parent, as a spouse, as a racial or ethnic minority. Such doubts always remain with us. Remnants of Cristina's educationally marginalized identity will always be a part of her newly forming, yet more competent and capable, identity as a successful student. It will serve as a reminder of her strengths, agency, and persistence. This day, she wanted some reassurance that I viewed her as a capable student, and that she would be successful. And since one's identity is also defined by how others perceive one (Holland et al., 1998), telling Cristina how I perceived her abilities in that moment contributed to how she defined herself. Her apprehension may have stemmed from the fact that she was no longer going to have the CAMP program support and human resources available to her in times of need and/or personal or academic crises. She was exhibiting some tendencies to waver in her trajectory as a student learning to be and become successful and feel confident about this way of being. But considering what she had accomplished, and the realizations of what she is capable of, Cristina will undoubtedly do well.

Cristina's mother saw her as a model of the possibilities in education. She too was empowered by Cristina's desire and determination, eventually enrolling in college herself. Cristina has even had an effect on other family members, telling me, "I see how me going to college has influenced my whole family. My mom's sister wants to go now. Just because they know now it's possible. Sometimes they don't even think about it." She also told me how the story of her experience and the possibilities in education reached others in the community.

> If I would have never come to college, my mom wouldn't have either. And I think I'm influencing other people, too, because I'm showing my mom that she can make it, and yet that was never a possibility for her in the past. Now, she told one of her coworkers, and he's a mechanic, and he says, yeah, I can't even read these labels. Ask your daughter if I can go to college, too. So now I have to get him an application, because they really want to go to school, but they just need somebody to push them. Now my mom's excited, now that her boss is excited too, that could have a really good outcome if my mom really learned English. Her boss says she could do so much, but she's not bilingual yet.

The sustaining effects of being a successful student in college through the CAMP program were passed through Cristina to her family and to the community. They saw her as a success story, which provided a model for opportunity through education and the hope found therein.

## Concluding Thoughts on Cristina's Change

Cristina had harbored the desire to attend college for quite some time. She said, "I really wanted to go to college, but deep down inside I knew that college wasn't an option. As a little girl, graduating [from high school] would be my biggest goal. That would be the best thing I could do for myself. College was not even in my thoughts." Somehow, she was socialized to believe academic or financial barriers would prevent her from ever going to college. Attending high school did not ameliorate this problem in her educational and life trajectory. She revealed how she took "basic classes" because she just wanted to finish high school and start working. She wished that the school "would have been a lot stricter and made you take all these classes. I know it's my fault, but I know they could have done something, and try to get you more involved, and make you understand." The school should have made more of an effort to, as Cristina put it, make the students "think" about college, and not just make superficial scholarship announcements or conduct insincere meetings about college. According to Cristina, not only was the school negligent in providing information and advice on the complexities of financial aid options available to students like Cristina, there was an apparent culture and pedagogy of inaccessibility for Mexicano students. Cristina briefly recalled that she was always with the Mexicanos and that there was an underlying belief that they would never have the chance to go to college.

The CAMP scholarship changed her life and educational trajectory. Financially, it was her "open door," and then it was a matter of giving her the chance to participate in school through the program. Although at times encountering various academic and language hurdles, she embodied a great sense of desire (and need) to succeed and take advantage of the many opportunities she was provided throughout the program, for which she constantly expressed her gratitude. Reflecting what Campa (2010) found in her study of resilient Latina/o community college students, Cristina not only wanted to be successful in college so that she could get a job that would allow her to buy her mother a new house. She was also driven by a larger purpose beyond herself—for her community and family. Specifically, she expressed how she wanted to be successful for the Chicano community. But her abusive father was also in the back of her mind, fueling much of her desire to succeed. She told me she wanted to "go and be a successful woman and go see him, because he used to always tell me that I was not going to be anything, and I thought I was this and that because I was born here, and I want to prove him wrong."

As part of the CAMP community, Cristina had access to and utilized all the human resources that were available to increase her chances of continuing her college education. As part of the community of teachers and learners, these people who were invested in Cristina's success provided her the information needed to remain on a trajectory toward becoming a more knowledgeable student in the ways of navigating the college institution. Cristina received coaching, encouragement, assistance in scholarship applications, financial aid, and English writing assignments. Those assisting Cristina not only equipped her with the cultural capital necessary to successfully make her way through classes and the financial obligations of college tuition, but also created interactional spaces that contributed to a sense of agency within her developing student identity. Lisa, the CAMP coordinator, was especially critical in this dynamic of her identity development. Cristina told me, "[Lisa] always believed in me. . . . So she tried to get me involved in everything and believed in me. Just her support, how much she believed in me, helped me a lot. It helped me develop who I am now." Cristina's use and repetition of the word *believe* indicates that someone like Lisa having faith in her abilities and her future possibilities was crucial in contributing to and maintaining a positive and confident sense of self.

The intensive support provided by the CAMP program was constant for an academic year but also reflected a Vygotskian approach to teaching grounded in his theory of learning that says that what students can do with assistance today, they will be able to do on their own tomorrow (Vygotsky, 1978). The courses, curriculum, and activities were created in a way to gradually assist the students from their distant peripheral positions in college culture and academics to being more independent and ready for college on their own. Cristina felt that the CAMP experience was an effective way to instill and reinforce notions of success through hard work, as well as a form of encouragement and faith in their future academic abilities. She knew that "that's what got you started and got you believing that it wasn't that hard and you could do it." Cristina had a sense that the community was created to keep her on a trajectory toward accomplishing individual, as well as group, goals. This constant reinforcement through her hard work, struggles, and many successes began to influence the way she perceived herself as a person and a student.

Cristina's chance to participate in the CAMP and college community was critical in her development and self-perception. She told me that this experience was the "one door, one opportunity, one chance, you know? And actually, giving me a chance . . . that made me also believe in myself, and that's why I'm here." Unlike her high school, which did not provide any entry point into communities or places of possibility in her educational trajectory, the CAMP program provided Cristina access to a community of practice to learn a successful student identity. This community engaged and motivated Cristina, and also equipped her with the tools to continue with her education, apprenticing her to the next levels of learning and understanding. Because she participated and succeeded in the practices, she was "changing my way of seeing myself. Now I see myself like I could accomplish anything, and I could do it. . . . I think that I have worked very hard in college for everything, so I see myself very differently." As such, Cristina sees her new identities. Confident and capable identities.

With her bilingual abilities, successful navigation of the college culture, and her abilities to overcome obstacles, Cristina represents Trueba's (2002) ideas on these abilities being salient parts of multiple identities in Latinas/os. And these abilities, he suggests, will be a part of a new cultural capital that future generations will embrace and utilize to be successful in the changing social and cultural paradigm of schools and society. Much of Cristina's success came because she was resilient and persistent, even in the face of challenges and doubt in her abilities. Cristina's success reflects what Gloria, Castellanos, and Orozco (2005) found in their study of college-going Latinas who resisted a fatalistic approach to dealing with schooling difficulties and the ability to adopt particular active strategies in dealing with such difficulties. Cristina developed not only new academic and cultural sensibilities about college, but a new sensibility of self and how this new way of being could work to her advantage in other aspects of college. And because she had experienced the intricacies of the college institution, culture, and academics by successfully completing the academic year, she felt more equipped when she began her second year of college. She told me, "I started to know how everything goes and how everything runs, and that's why I'm okay this year."

# Luz: "It's hard . . . working outside in the sun"

James saw that Luz evolved in expressing herself in small-group discussions and in her interactions with others. He said there were "some changes in maturity or the way that she would present herself. I felt in the first quarter, she was very reserved, kind of in the background, relied on a small group of friends quite a bit to be a buffer or to diffuse responsibility and things like that." To James, Luz was developing a sense of openness to the world, and not relying on being hidden behind or within groups of others. She was feeling more comfortable in expressing her developing sense of self in classroom practice and interactions with others.

Lisa also saw Luz change in her manner of interacting. Initially, Luz was seen as someone who "thought she would be a total loner." However, according to Lisa, Luz "found herself being asked for help, and then I think she gave it a try, and she figured out she was good at it. She became a Spanish tutor for Bobby, and he asked her for help, and she said yes. She said okay. She was good at it. She doesn't get close to people; she keeps her distance, she's tough. She did soften a little bit; I would say she did." Luz developed as a more socially interactive person, who initially would close herself off to most of the world. Through communication and productive interactions with others, she discovered new aspects of her personality and her capabilities as person, student, and, in this case, teacher. She discovered that she could have other types of relationships, in this case with a man, and not have to fear such relationships interfering with her own objectives and trajectory.

Throughout most of the year in the program, Luz typically worked alone on her projects and assignments for class, unless instructed to do otherwise. In the following field notes, I was in the Computer/Career Planning Learning Community observing the students working on assignments for class at their computers. It was an individually assigned task, with the option of working with others. While most of the students were working alone, I found Luz working with another student on the assignment: "Some of the students, like Juan and Luz, are helping each other with their project. Most of the work by others in the class is being done individually, with little collaboration; most of the time, if the student needs some help, they call on the instructor to ask for help. This is unusual because Luz typically works alone. She has tended to work alone most of the year." This behavior was vastly different from how Luz would interact with others in the group on academic assignments during the year. She would participate in the activities she was obligated to participate in, such as Adventure Learning, but would not work with others on school work. She developed at a social level where she interacted more with others and found benefits in doing so in the form of getting assistance with classwork.

Luz mentioned that she was doing something out of the norm for a woman in her family. That her sisters had married immediately after high school, had children, worked in low-paying jobs, and did not go to college was one of the major driving forces behind Luz's seeking a college education. She felt empowered to do something different with her life. She not only wanted to do something different from her sisters; she wanted to prove to her male friends and past romantic interests that she could be somebody different.

> I want to show them that I can . . . all the guy friends, Mexican friends, all the boyfriends I've had, they always said, yeah, you're going to get married and this and that, whatever. I just basically want to show them, you know, that I can go on. I'm not going to screw up my life with these . . . because my ex-boyfriends wanted me to live with them and this and that. I said, no, I'm not that stupid. I have an education still. And I was still in high school. All I planned to do when I was dating them, I just wanted to finish high school. That's all I expected—for them to wait for me, just let me finish high school, that's all I'm asking for. Now that I've finished high school, now I say, well, you guys wait until I get my nursing degree, until I get my associate's, bachelor's, or whatever I want to get.

The pressure of romance and relationships was always there for Luz. But Luz resisted not only this discourse but the advances and proposals of young men desiring a commitment. Her ambitions for a profession and advanced degrees are weapons for her in this tension.

One skill that Luz suggested she had learned and brought over from her experiences in CAMP was that of being able to better relate to and interact with the world around her. The CAMP experience seemed to open her up to communicating with others and feeling more comfortable and confident in being around people in her classes and in her surroundings in general.

> I think I've improved my shyness. Before, I wouldn't talk to teachers, or I wouldn't ask questions. I wouldn't talk to anybody who was sitting beside me. It was like, no, I never would talk to anybody. It was just me and I'd figure out things on my own. Now with CAMP, we were all together, we would ask questions to each other. I just felt more confident in myself, and I just didn't feel shy anymore around people. It just opened me up. Now that I'm at Front Range [another community college], I'm with new students and professors, and I ask them questions. I talk to them like it's nothing. And before I would never do that, so, that's probably what CAMP did for me. . . . That changed me totally, yeah, in communicating with other people. Don't ask me how that happened, but yeah, it did happen. I noticed that, because I'll talk to anybody now.

Furthermore, Luz realized that if she didn't even approach others about questions she may have about, for example, school, class work, or financial aid, then she would not be able to get far in trying to deal with problems or academic issues. "I feel more comfortable, because before, I was like, if I don't have questions, then where am I going to get to if I'm not willing to ask them? It helped me. Because, my work, if I don't understand it, how am I going to get it if I don't ask the teacher what is this? So yes, it helps me."

For Luz, success was a matter of "getting things accomplished." After completing a year of college, she was confident that she could continue to effectively deal with adversity and work hard to reach her goals.

> Because the way I looked at it at the beginning of the year was that if I could get the year accomplished successfully, then I could go on after that. Now that I've done a year, now I know I can do three or four or five more. The years go flying, I've noticed. If I could get through this year, then I could go on. If I

don't, then I'm not going to go on. Now I look at it as if, when something happens and I can only go halfway, or not finish another year, I know that after that problem is over, whatever, I can still continue with school. Because if I finish this year, why can't I finish the others?

Luz looked back on the school year, as well as on her life, especially the times of working in the fields as a young girl. Even with struggles, she realized that "if those things had not happened, you know, you pass through experience in order to learn things. So, if those things happened for a reason, well, they happened because it's destiny." From her life and from her recent schooling experiences, she learned that

I'm strong. I don't put myself to fail very easily. I have lots of strength, I really do, because I have been through a lot. Now that I look at people who work in the fields, all my memories go back to when I used to work. It's like, oh my God, I used to be like that. I don't know, in a way there's . . . I sometimes feel like going to work there again just to feel again what it was to be like that. I still remember, but I just want to feel more like . . . I would like for them to know that they can succeed even though they're working in the fields.

Luz confessed that a part of what she was doing—going to college, working her way toward a nursing degree—was motivated by how she felt when she worked in the fields, remembering her family endure the physical pain of quickly fillings bags with a crop to meet a quota, and still seeing people her age doing that work today. She garnered strength and determination from her life as a migrant worker. But she wanted those still working in the fields to know that they can still have aspirations beyond the fields. Luz wanted her present position and identity as a successful student and Latina to be a message to those who may be losing hope of getting out of the fields and into the college classroom—that it is possible. The college classroom just seemed easier for Luz. And she knew from experience, "because you know . . . it's hard working outside in the sun."

## Concluding Thoughts on Luz's Change

Luz's identity as a student and potential professional as a nurse was battling a discourse of romance, relationships, and domesticity. With all her older sisters already having gotten pregnant at a young age, getting married and raising their children, there was a pattern in her immediate family that she did not want to follow. This influenced her attitude toward college throughout high school and even immediately after. She stated that she "just wanted to finish high school and that was it, just like my sisters did. I didn't want to go to college, what for?"

Her marginalization stemmed from internal conflicts of identity, gender roles, and purpose, much of the conflict fueled by words of discouragement from relatives in Mexico. With over half the academic year complete, Luz had a fatalistic view of her life in romance and relationships. As shown by her "letter to young self" that the CAMP students wrote in their Career Planning learning community course, she feared that love would lead to marriage and children, taking her away from her college aspirations: "The first thing is don't fall in love and let a guy take you away from what you are doing now. Don't let anything overcome you. Keep on fighting until your dreams become a reality." Luz believed that going to college and marriage with children were mutually exclusive.

Even though Luz made fairly good grades throughout high school, she still didn't see herself as "smart," but more as hardworking. She thought that college could not be for someone like her, because college was only for particular types that fit a certain mold. People, however, began to enter her life and influence her self-perception as a capable student. It was apparent that various key interactions and relationships with encouraging educators and more knowledgeable others were contributing to her agency and trajectory toward being and becoming a successful student. Teachers in high school, for example, saw potential in her and perhaps even sensed her apathy toward her future and higher education. She said that one high school teacher in particular, Ms. Rivas, was especially integral to Luz's trajectory toward and participation in college. Throughout her CAMP experience, Luz was still exposed to and had access to people invested in her as a presently and potentially successful student. She cited a good relationship with a college adviser, Israel, and the help and advice she received from a learning community instructor, Cinthia.

Luz's immediate family was supportive of her educational pursuits. This family support motivated her and contributed to her agency, which reflects what Ceja (2004) found on the various role(s) that parental support played in the determination and resilience of Chicana college students. One of the salient points made by Ceja's (2004) study is that parents supported their college-going daughters in different ways—directly and indirectly. This is contrary to the deficit view that Mexican-descent families do not value education or do not encourage their children to go to college (Valencia and Black, 2002). For example, in her study of Latina/o community college students, Zell (2010) found that the family and parents of Latina/o students supported them by offering concrete support such as child care, or even making a quick breakfast to eat before class. Luz expressed her joy in getting such support from her family, especially her father, that "it makes me feel good when they tell people I'm in college to become a nurse. They're positive and sure about me. They know I'll become what I want to become. I think that has helped me the most, more than anything else in college." Reflecting the power of moral support for Latina students (Auerbach, 2006), Luz felt that the support from her parents was the greatest factor in helping her to stay in college and remain confident in her trajectory toward her goals.

Luz learned a number of other things during her CAMP experience. Among them, that her interactions with others and relationships with adult role models helped her to be more personable, to ask more questions, and to seek out help when needed. She also learned about the intricacies of college life, culture, and institutional navigation from these invested others. And although this new knowledge helped her navigate successfully, her college experience was tainted with tension. She feared romance leading to marriage getting in the way of her goals. She knew she didn't want to be a wife and mother right away, but having a serious boyfriend and unsupportive relatives did not help her decision. Coupled with the support from her parents, her participation in the CAMP community and access to interactions with people like Israel helped her deal with her situation. This helped her maintain her trajectory toward her goals, which reassured her successful student identity, and Luz continued to do well.

## Maria: "I don't want to quit"

Jane, Maria's math instructor, talked about how Maria struggled with the content in her class but eventually changed in how she handled the coursework. She said that Maria "had a hard time with math. She really struggles with it. At the beginning she was just blowing it off and saying, 'Maybe it's too hard for me, I just won't come in to class.' But she's kind of had a different change of attitude this quarter. Now she says, 'I know I have to get this done, I know I have to work harder on it than I did before.' So she's becoming more focused on it, working harder on it." Maria exhibited perseverance in the face of academic difficulty. Jane noticed that Maria sometimes struggled to get to class, early in the term. But she observed how, in the next quarter, Maria's attitude and efforts seemed changed. It appeared that Maria realized her need to make decisions that would allow her to manage more effectively her identities as mother and student.

Lisa felt that Maria, through her successes and struggles in school, learned a great deal about the nature of managing the difficulties and responsibilities of college, and what she needed to do to pursue her career goals. She said that Maria "did grow a lot as far as understanding what she needs to do to go where she wants to go. She did take steps to become a dental assistant, apply for a job, so she's trying to get her foot in the door for the thing that she wants to do. So I was proud of that. She took lots of good steps. She grew in understanding the plan, what she needs to do, the vastness of it—she kind of got a grasp of that." From Lisa's perspective, Maria displayed an understanding of mapping her life and school career effectively. She was developing a sensibility of self that recognized the need to tap into various networks and sources of information in college and beyond.

Maria began to struggle academically after her first quarter, especially with writing and math. She was juggling her responsibilities at home with her children and family and her schoolwork, often distressed about how to manage everything effectively. The following field notes of Maria in an English workshop illustrate that Maria learned to take advantage of the academic support services available. She also recognized that how she managed her use of time within particular contexts—in school versus at home—was essential for her academic success.

Maria is working with William on her paper outline. She is working diligently on it. I ask her about why she attends the English workshop, and she says, "It's extra help. I mean for me, I go home and I don't have the time. I don't have time to do everybody's homework. He [William] suggested I do my work here because it would be easier for me" and that in the workshop, she mentions how "it is easier for me to do it here and to have him [William] right here when I need immediate help. So, to me, I think it's really helpful."

Maria felt that being a CAMP scholar began to change her personality, making her more social and communicative with others.

I think it's helped me to become a better person. I used to be very quiet; now I just talk and talk, that's all I do. I used to be really shy, embarrassed, and now I'm like, whatever, who cares. My mom tells me that too. She says I act different now, funnier. My sisters are like, "Did you just see what she did?" and I'm like, "What did I do?" My personality has changed; my mom and everybody else sees it, too. I think it's helping me feel better about myself and not to be so shy around other people.

Maria began to feel empowered to be who she really wanted to be, to be more comfortable and confident, and to have the freedom to express it to and around others. She appeared to break through her "shyness," also revealing a more comedic side of her personality because now she was "funnier."

After attending two academic quarters, she felt like she was partly successful and partly not, because she had to withdraw from the last quarter. She began to cry when thinking about what she accomplished and what she could have accomplished had she not left the program early to attend to her family obligations: "I've succeeded because I'm happier and because I know . . . quitting . . . I'm like half and half. I don't consider myself successful. No. Because I quit. [Crying] Just that it's hard. It's not hard for everybody, but in my position, I think it's hard, with my kids and all. I just quit. I didn't finish my whole year. I don't think that's successful, quitting." Maria begins by stating she is happier, but she is not quite sure what she is happy about. Her tone, after hesitation and some thought, changes to one of disappointment, perhaps because she recognizes the reality of her current life situation. She realizes that being a young, single mother of two will not make going to college easy, something she knows that so many others do not have to experience. To Maria, because she quit, at this moment, she did not think she was successful in college.

After more conversation and some time for Maria to reflect further on her experience in college through CAMP, she began to sound determined. She said that she would continue with her education. Having participated in college and understanding the realities of it, she felt prepared for any adversity she could encounter the next time she attends. She said, "I see what it's like now. I didn't consider it was going to be that hard. Having my kids and all. I went through the beginning okay; then it was getting harder and harder. So I know what it's like now."

Maria said that she learned, after having been with a cohort of supportive staff and students, that she could continue on her own. It was a matter of realizing her own potential in and through her efforts, and maintaining a desire to individually persevere.

> I learned that I can do it even though I don't have all the CAMP students with me or you or Lisa. I know that I can still do it as long as I try. I can keep going. At first, we said, "What are we going to do without you guys?" We're like all together. And then we're thinking, "Well, we have to." We have to move on by ourselves. We can't always carry everybody in a little bag and carry them with us when we go to school and finish.

Maria also expressed that, because of having experienced the difficulties of college the way she did, she learned insightful and practical knowledge about herself as a student and mother. She told me, "I feel proud of myself. I actually went to college," and insisted that she would use this experience to come back and continue on her trajectory toward being and becoming a successful student. Maria found her experience in college through CAMP as one in which having her children and being a young, single mother was "part of a larger, more complex picture, not the end of a story" (Schultz, 2001, p. 588).

I think it's because I've already experienced it and then I quit, and I took some time to think about it. Now I know that I can. I don't think that if I come, then I'm going to let myself down again, because I have to take it slow. I can't do some things, like take three classes when I know I can't, so I'll maybe try two or one with something that I'm going to be comfortable with and be able to do it so I don't just quit. I don't want to quit.

## Concluding Thoughts on Maria's Change

Maria's educational marginalization was exacerbated by a life situation of thousands of teenage girls in the United States every year—dropping out of high school due to pregnancy and stigmatization (Allen, Philliber, Herrling, and Kuperminc, 1997). Announcing her pregnancy to her father and family was difficult and life-changing. She was forced to drop out of high school and enroll in a GED program. Because she struggled with her academics while needing to take care of her children, it took her two years to earn her GED.

She was not necessarily nervous about going to college and taking college-level courses; rather, she was more excited and ready for what she saw as a good opportunity. The formation of a positive sense of self and her potential as a student began even before she started the program. She felt that she had accomplished a great deal by simply being accepted into the CAMP program. This acceptance was her entrance into a new community of possibility.

Maria often felt like her college experience was a bit surreal because, she told me, she never imagined herself in college, after her pregnancies, being a single mother, and the situation with her father. Early in the program, she could not visualize herself as a student, much less a successful student doing college work. Although she struggled with her coursework, she still managed to get three As (in non-content, college-level credit courses) and a B and a C (in content, math and English, developmental courses) in her first quarter as a college student.

This initial success with her academics encouraged her self-perception as a capable student. Being a part of a community of other students who struggled together and assisted one another also contributed to the agency within her trajectory toward this sense of accomplishment. Maria began to tire, though, as the multiple outside responsibilities she had, along with the increasing difficulty of the courses, mounted and created a great deal of pressure for her. Late in her second quarter in college, days before the end of the year, her mother was no longer able to care for her children. The outside pressures and complexities of family and responsibilities, despite the supportive nature and community of her schooling experiences in CAMP, could not be overcome.

Maria had no choice but to withdraw from the program days before the end of the year. Although she was still a part of a community of practice in school and was experiencing academic success, Maria's life outside of school was a powerful influence in her trajectory in the CAMP program. She was on two trajectories within two communities of practice, her life with her children and her school life, which were difficult for her to merge into a mutual dynamic. Similar to the teen mothers in Zachry's (2005) study who honestly and openly admitted that their current situation would be a challenge in the pursuit of higher education, Maria was well aware of how difficult life would be. But despite having to withdraw from the program, she learned what would be necessary for her to successfully navigate the difficulty of being a young, single mother while attending college.

The act of engaging in college and the practice of being a student served as the impetus for Maria to realize she could continue with her schooling. In that sense, Maria was very successful as a college student. She discovered that she could do college when she earned good grades. She acquired a sense of belonging to a community of learners, where her personality blossomed through collaboration and interaction with others. Maria also realized another level of maturity and experience to her identity as a mother and a student, two complicated life trajectories that, only at this moment, could not coexist for her. Maria did not know *how* to make them coexist. But, as we found with Maria, she was determined to make these two trajectories and communities of practice coexist and work to her benefit as an aspiring dental assistant.

Schultz (2001) found that teen mothers often spoke in empowering discourses about their experiences as young mothers. Like Maria, they wanted to use their lives and current situations as points of departure toward realizing a future they wanted for themselves and their children. Schultz (2001) argued that "if as educators and policymakers we recognize that early childbearing and motherhood *can* become a motivating factor in young women's lives rather than a source of despair, we can explicitly address the students from this understanding and help them to plan their lives accordingly" (p. 604). The power of Maria's experience and discourse is in her aspirations and determination to make her life work the ways she wants it to. Indeed, she has come from a place of despair when she first discovered her pregnancy—"I just wanted to stop"—but has made significant movement from marginalization by having practiced and knowing what it is to be a successful student.

## Ruben: "I was caught between two worlds"

The struggles for Ruben began early in the year. He talked to me extensively about adjusting to school and his new life:

> I'm having a conversation with Ruben outside of the Psychology/Master Student class. We are sitting together at a small, round table that the students usually sit at to study or eat or just hang out with others. It is just outside of the class that is presently being conducted, Psychology and Master Student. He talks to me about how he is struggling with the class, and with some life issues. He mentions how the other day he was passing by a car with its window open, and he is tempted to steal the purse, but he doesn't. He looks at me intently, through his scratched glasses, and tells me how painful it was to actually do that, to not steal the purse. He tells me he has been tempted many times to "go back to his old ways," like back in "the hood," during his days of gang-banging. But he no longer participates as fully as he once did. He is tempted once in a while. He sometimes engages in activities that keep him on the boundary between his old ways, and the ways of being a student, trying to learn how to learn and be a good student, something he was deprived of in high school. He tells me that he wants a new life. He wants to change, get a real job, get some respect.

This vignette illustrates Ruben's enduring struggle of identities as he was initially experiencing college. The history and experience that made up who and what he was conflicted with his cultural and personal knowledge of how to participate in the college and CAMP community of practice. His situational marginalization of the gang life and peer group was still a strong part of his life and lingered within his new schooling trajectory. Ruben's desire to seek out others in a different social and educational context reflected his willingness to confess to his struggles in choosing between right and wrong. This may have indicated his struggles in transitioning to an alternate personal, social, and cultural world that was now part of his schooling. His interactions with others were influencing his creation of new ways of being and thinking within this college and CAMP community of practice. But it was difficult for him.

James talked about how he saw Ruben change slightly in the ways that he understood the nature of college. He admitted that Ruben had to still learn the nature of responsibility with doing the coursework, suggesting that "on a practical level there wasn't a whole lot of change . . . how he went about managing himself in terms of the coursework was very similar in the first quarter to this quarter." Ruben mishandled his work responsibilities in school and wavered on the outer edge of the periphery of the community of practice throughout the entire year, not showing much growth. James felt that Ruben exhibited the same habits throughout the year, not being able to maintain a stable sense of doing the work necessary to be successful in his class.

Lisa knew that Ruben was not academically successful in this college experience, but she thought he might have taken away some other valuable lessons that became a new and profound aspect of who he was and was becoming.

> It was a learning experience . . . academically it wasn't fully successful. I think the social part of it was valuable. When you're in a gang, your social skills just aren't what they are supposed to be for regular life, and I think that what he gained out of the year was really valuable reality social skills. With real people, everyday life, how to treat people, how to talk in regular situations, in a classroom, so I think he grew a lot that way. Because

he didn't know how to do that stuff. When he first came he was really abrasive, loud, and didn't know how to control himself. I think he learned a lot about that. And he softened a lot. You saw him with Bobby's little girls; he was just so fun with them and kind to them, and I think having to be tough all the time was hard on him. He grew up way too early.

Because Lisa was able to get to know Ruben very well on personal and academic levels, she became aware of his struggles inside and outside of school. Lisa observed how valuable the social adaptation to this schooling context was for Ruben's development and learning. She believed that Ruben had been sheltered from the "regular life" of schooling and community, which isolated him from social and academic contexts that would provide opportunities to interact with others in a positive manner and realize a new sense of self.

After completing most of the academic year, Ruben felt he was changing but was unsure about the ways he saw himself in the college world and being a college student. He confessed that the transition in coming from a "cholo gang life" and attending college was "weird, because I'm feeling like an outsider in both areas now." He admitted that he had been learning something from the CAMP experience and being in college. To him, though, it was more about simply being there that contributed to a positive sense of self and what he was doing with his life. He said, "I saw myself as a changed person. I see it not as a college student, but as a person trying to succeed in life, not only succeeding in college." Ruben expressed how he saw himself as "somewhat successful" as a student the past year. He said that it wasn't about numbers or good grades but "to do the best you can. Whether you made it or not, that don't matter. As long as you tried your best."

School for Ruben was a battle of ways of being in different worlds. The gravity of the demands on his competing identities was taxing. He was attempting to get away from negative influences and fit in a world and structure (college) that he could not completely conceive himself existing in:

I was caught between two worlds. My homeboys were all cholo, and I wanted to get out, and now, to me, I don't even consider myself that. I see myself as my own person now, not a cholo. I'm not a college student, I'm not a cholo, I'm me. With all that struggling, I had to psych myself. What complicated things was that here I wanted to go to college, but here I had homeboys and all that other stuff. My mind was still torn, and it took a lot of thinking and struggling, and now that I found a place where I'm finally happy in who I am, I ain't struggling no more.

Ruben was unsure of his place in school and being in college. At that point in the year he was fighting against history and life experience that had created who he was going into this new experience of a positive and additive environment.

He suggested that this past year was making him more focused in his direction in school and life, feeling more confident in his abilities and the possibilities.

> Even though I was struggling, it was good. You know, college? Even though I didn't make perfect grades, I learned a lot from it and felt like I did well for all the shit I was going through, I did well for what I could do, and it opened my eyes up to see once I feel confident in myself with my foundation, I know I can do it, now I know I can. Now that it's there, that's what I'm saying, it's because the CAMP program has taught me a lesson of what to look for when I go back.

Ruben expressed a deeper knowledge of his struggling identity of self, and developing student identity through adversity in school and life. Because he experienced college in this way, he said, "Now I know what college is and what I really need to do, what mind frame I need to be in."

A few months after the end of CAMP, Ruben moved to California with his family. He was working with a computer company that installs machinery and computer programs for small businesses and grocery store chains. He mentioned that he was one from a large pool of applicants hired as a full-time employee with benefits, mainly because he had told his boss that he had college experience. His boss told him that it showed he had determination and reflected positively on him. Ruben said he wanted to study computer science and would be pursuing his degree the next year, after he established state residency. He also mentioned that the company he works for would pay for his tuition as long as he commits to them after he receives his degree, which influenced his decision to pursue computer science. He thought that his having participated in college might have influenced his boss to hire him. He said, "I told my boss that I did do a year; it showed some kind of determination, so that he said, yeah, I'll hire you. I told him that I wanted to go back to computer science, and he said, yeah, definitely. So, me going to college did a lot of things. It really helped me out in some ways."

Ruben said that the people involved in his experiences as a first-year college student influenced his perception of the potential that people have. It made him realize that people can change, despite their history or background, and, as he did, can learn what it takes to accomplish goals: "It was the people that were involved. Also the fact that I knew that, no matter where you come from, you can still go to college and better yourself. You can do things and still come up. It taught me a lot of things. I learned actually some responsibility, you know what I mean? Having to go to school every day, that wasn't like me, so I learned a lot of responsible things from going to college."

Ruben felt that one of the most important things he took from his experiences in the CAMP program and his first year in college was that despite what the world may think about you, success is still possible when you accept who you are. He realized that everyone in the CAMP cohort accepted one another and worked and contributed to a trajectory toward a different life or educational goal: "Yes, I just want to be . . . I can be who I am and what I do shows respect for myself. That's what I pretty much learned from them, like everybody was different, everybody got along, so many different people got together, and they made something. They were all kind of going for the same goal . . . an education."

## Concluding Thoughts on Ruben's Change

A few months after the end of that year's CAMP program, Ruben contacted the CAMP office and I spoke with him again about how life was going for him. He wanted to talk to the coordinator of the

CAMP program, just to let her know how he was doing. We spoke for awhile and he asked about several of the former CAMP students. I sensed a hint of longing for those students, his friends and classmates, and what they meant to him throughout his first-year college experience. He wanted to know if I had seen them around campus or in the CAMP office. I told him no, to which he sighed, a bit disappointed. I sensed that he hoped that things were going well for his friends and former classmates, as they were for him—with a good job, or attending college, or planning on doing something, anything, good with their lives—just like him.

Ruben's historical marginalization in school and society was a deeply ingrained part of his identity and created conflicting forces within his college trajectory entering the CAMP program. He felt that in his identity "there were confrontations, because there would be times where I'm two halves trying to co-exist. I feel like I have an angel and a devil on my shoulder. I'm like, you need to study to get your education, you need to do that essay. The devil, says, fuck that essay, you need to go out with your homeboys and get drunk! It's a big conflict." And although excited about the idea of going to college, he wasn't even sure that it was the right choice for him at the time, saying his feelings about it were "more like confused, you know, like, is this really for me? You know, like, do I even, you know, should I even do it?" His identity as a "cholo" and the dynamics that accompanied it in his first-year college experience often created obstacles for his trajectory into the communities of practice within the CAMP program and goals of actively engaging and taking on the identity(ies) of being and becoming a successful student (R. Reyes, 2006).

Ruben was having trouble allowing what he was learning in CAMP to change or empower him to change. This reflects what Harris and Shelswell (2005) found in their study of communities of practice in adult basic education (ABE). They suggest there is risk of continued marginalization and disempowerment of participants if they do not learn to integrate what they have learned from their communities into their daily lives. The history of the practice of being a gang member impeded the present learning of the practice of being a CAMP student, a dynamic that Wenger (1998) suggested would occur for individuals when membership in one community turns into marginalization in the other. In the case of Ruben, his marginalization in society as a gang member made it difficult for full membership in the CAMP community of practice. Even though away from his original gang peer group, that history was still a part of who he was when he still attracted friends from similar backgrounds after he moved to Colorado.

Ruben suggested having found a sense of agency and trajectory in his academic, professional, and personal life through this experience. Because of the present obsession with standards, numbers reflecting learning and success, and leaving no child behind, the mainstream definition of success would be considered vastly different from how Ruben defined it. Ruben saw that he was successful by at least having had the opportunity to participate in and be a part of an institution of higher education and trying his best. Not meeting the CAMP contract requirements of maintaining a 2.0 GPA, along with lack of class attendance and completing course requirements, may be seen as Ruben's inability to fulfill academic obligations in the college, and one could conclude that he was a "failure." Ruben saw it radically differently. He saw the CAMP experience as a personal test of will. The actual, physical act of being in school and at the college was a success in and of itself, quite different from his past educational experiences. Ruben's trajectory was not imagined. Being in CAMP and going to college was an affirmation of his existence. It was a step in a new direction for his life and education, changing his trajectory and sense of self, a sense of being and becoming. Going to college was an experience of the possible for him. He only needed more time.

## Concluding Thoughts on All Students: Who They Are, Became, and Are Becoming

Wenger (1998) believes that "education in its deepest sense, and at whatever age it takes place, concerns the opening of identities—exploring new ways of being that lie beyond our current state" (p. 263). Indeed, college through CAMP allowed movement beyond the students' state of marginalization. And in this movement and practice they discovered who and what they were at that moment, and who and what they could become. The program in which the students participated functioned as a chance, an opportunity, a point of access to a place and experience that their marginalization probably would have prevented them from gaining under normal societal circumstances, which reward individualism and "pulling oneself up by one's bootstraps." The scholarship itself provided the entry point to a world that would not have been possible for most of these students. It was entry into a world, a community of teaching and learning, in which they had the freedom and support to explore the possibilities in new identities, new ways of being. For these students, the CAMP program and its one year of financial, academic, and personal support represented redemption, a second chance at proving their worth as students.

Similar to Gándara's (1995) findings of her educationally mobile student case studies, the role of structured opportunity, such as financial aid or a recruitment program, was critical for students in this study in the form of the CAMP scholarship. They probably would not have had a similar opportunity elsewhere. Most of Gándara's case studies, however, already had positive and strong identities as students going into college. Most of the students in her study had already proven their capabilities in school, through hard work, ambition, outstanding academic records, and the like. The students in this study, however, were hindered by some form of marginalization that was inhibiting academic performance and complete investment in their educational pursuits. There were sociocultural issues, inside and outside school, that influenced their identities as capable, motivated, and determined students, and lacked a great deal of agency to maintain a positive trajectory toward being and becoming successful students. Because each student enacted a sense of habitus in his or her practice by overcoming any limits of prior marginalization, the students' movement and learning through the CAMP program reflected a capacity to generate their own actions and products of success (Bourdieu, 1990). Each student in this study ended up at some point beyond his or her marginalization, but with a new realized self and self-determined and self-defined understanding of success.

Like so many other situationally marginalized students in our schools today, these students each took their histories and present cultural and home situations to their college life, which created various tensions of struggle and success in school. The student participation in a community of practitioners and educators was influenced by notions of experience, support and encouragement, and possibility. There were invested others of the CAMP program, such as instructors, staff, and advisers, who were well versed in the ways of doing college and traversing various social and academic hardships that resonated with the students' present experiences. These people were invested in the lives and educations of the CAMP students. Students such as Cristina were able to deal more effectively with the challenges that college posed for them by accessing the support networks and the many people involved. The support and encouragement provided by Lisa, the coordinator, for example, was a driving force for Cristina, fueling her agency and belief in her abilities and the possibilities for her future. Ruben thought that his peer network was critical in helping to keep him in his educational trajectory and to stay in the program as long as possible. Maria appreciated such support networks, but realized that the complexity of life could overpower such efforts to help her stay in and do well in college. Laura recognized the support networks in the community, and appreciated the fact that the social interaction made her more open and social with others, but her agency came from determination and success in her coursework. Luz was always on an academic trajectory but internalized fears of romantic relationships impeding her progress. She did seek out counsel from people such as Israel, who helped to keep her focused, positive, and on track.

All students mentioned that their actual participation in college, and having the opportunity to participate in it, taught them something about being and becoming a successful college student. Similarly, Zell (2010) found that the Latinas in her study achieved a great sense of self-efficacy when they had the opportunity to attend college and succeed, despite low expectations from past teachers and their high schools. In this study, the actual practice of being a student was crucial in their development as students, through struggles and successes. As they succeeded, they learned about what it took to be successful and contributed to their agency while they gained momentum in their educational trajectory. If they struggled in their practice as students, they still acquired valuable skills by learning what *not* to do and gained a point of reference for future endeavors as a student or learner. If they had not had the chance at such practice, they would not have learned, mirroring Lave and Wenger's (1991) assertion that "denying access and limiting the centripetal movement of newcomers and other practitioners changes the learning curriculum" (p. 123).

Teachers recognize change in students. William has been a writing instructor at Next Step Community College for over a decade. He had seen many programs and projects, and worked with many students of varying academic abilities. After working with this cohort of CAMP students, he reflected,

> It seems to me pretty evident that something is helping these CAMP students advance more visibly than some of our regular students. Too often I think students leave here the same person that they were, without having developed personally. I think what I'm saying is that some CAMP students are good at doing that personal transformation that they need. It's not just academics; it's a whole mind-set, a whole self-perception, and whole self-understanding. I think the CAMP program is making a major difference. That has to be part of an explanation. What about the program's working to make that happen? I think there has to be something about the CAMP program that has promoted that kind of transformational change in some of these students.

The CAMP students participated in a program that promoted a philosophy and action of being successful by engaging in the various activities, classes, interactions and relationships within the CAMP community of practice. But they also practiced (or attempted to) not only what was required of the program to be successful, but what was required of themselves to go beyond educational, personal, and societal marginalization. For Latinos, knowing how to overcome their place of marginalization is often a "process of self-discovery" and "breaking away from internalized messages about their worth as individuals and students" (Zell, 2010, p. 171). For the marginalized, this process is part of their developing identity as successful students. Developing an identity and acting on that developed identity were two intermingled and inseparable parts of what it was to learn in situated contexts through movement beyond their marginalization. Doing and being are one and the same, because the student becomes as he or she does, going beyond the margins, the periphery, or where he or she was before having begun to engage in that act. When the CAMP students engaged in that act, they performed it (some more than others), whether it was modeled to them or explicitly taught. These acts involved taking on various characteristics of the identity of being and becoming a successful student. All the students in the study seemed to find success in various aspects of their performances as students, carrying this experience with them as a new and developing part of who they were and what they could become.

# 7

## *Discussion*

## Implications of the Possible

THE INTERACTIONAL DYNAMICS that occur in the educational contexts we construct for our students provide them opportunities to create a vision of what is possible within. With the CAMP program acting as a mediating force in the practice and performance of marginalized Mexican American students in their first year of college, we saw the possible in the power and impact of human interactions, relationships, and community on student identity and academic performance. We saw the possible in providing opportunities for the once-marginalized when they gained access to a community and then engaged in the practice and movement toward learning to be a successful student.

This study looked at the CAMP student experience through the conceptual frame of the learning of identity through practice and movement from a peripheral position in a community of practice toward learning to be and become more engaged and competent members (Lave and Wenger, 1991). One of the principal goals of such practice and movement is to acquire the characteristics of the target learning goal within the community of practice. In this case, the CAMP students were learning what was required to be successful as college students. They learned from CAMP personnel, instructors, mentors, and one another, reflecting Lave and Wenger's (1991) ideas on the importance of interactions with others in learning. The students learned and acquired practical knowledge and skills needed for academic persistence and success. But the CAMP students also learned how to utilize the human interactional dynamics in their networks and relationships and transform them into motivation and empowerment to fuel their agency and resilience. There were key interactions with various members of this community of practice that engaged them in the co-construction of knowing, understanding, empowerment, and persistence. Although these key interactions occurred *within* the movement from the periphery of their marginal existence, they also *drove* the movement—the learning and acquisition of characteristics of a successful student identity—itself.

Lave and Wenger (1991) see learning as practice, learning as identity. According to Wenger (1998), education should first begin with considering student identities and providing a sense of belonging in a community of practice. The CAMP program accomplished this. But, considering this way of looking at learning, how do we quantify the learning of successful student identities by marginalized students? Consider that not all of the students successfully completed their first year of college through CAMP, per the traditional and socially constructed and American sense of success (Varenne and McDermott, 1998). Despite all of the support, it just wasn't sufficient to help students like Maria and Ruben complete their first year of college with an adequate GPA and the readiness to move on to the next year of college. But understanding success is relative. Who is defining success? And for whom is success being defined? Both Maria and Ruben expressed how they still felt they were successful to some degree. Winning the CAMP scholarship was a symbol of success. Their physical presence and practice of being a student in college helped them to know success. In their eyes, they were successful.

Considering the way that student learning and experience was conceptually framed here, how Ruben and Maria perceived success has implications for the learner and the teacher, as well as for pundits and policy makers. For these marginalized students, their self-defined place of success represents *movement away from their initial places of marginalization in school and society*. They engaged in the practice of student and contributed to this movement with the agency created among themselves and those within the CAMP community of practice. They were given access to a community of practice that was different from the communities from which they came, and they embraced it. They were empowered by their participation, practice, and this movement. For marginalized students like Ruben or Maria, the initial attainment of stellar grades or high GPAs did not represent academic success. Grades are the institutionally defined part of the end result of such a process of learning to be a successful student. But Ruben and Maria had not arrived at that point in their movement within the community of practice. They were engaged in learning other, intangible ways of knowing and understanding themselves and their places in the college world, juxtaposed but also overlapping with the other communities of practice from which they came.

For Ruben and Maria, as well as the other CAMP students, it is the movement from their peripheral spaces that hints at the pedagogical possibilities in engaging and empowering marginalized student populations. There is pedagogy in this movement. Learning, development, and new understanding(s) come from this movement. In this sense, similar to Vygotsky's (1978) idea of the zone of proximal development, in which the learning process precedes the developmental processes, learning and the formation of identity occurred *before* the action of practice. The movement from a marginalized space reflects a type of learning internalized and emerging through present struggles and formation of identity *before* a marginalized student engages in the practice of learning how to be and become a successful student. But this movement is still success. It is the foundation of a successful student identity. Slight or even significant movement from a marginalized position within a community of practice is success for a student because it is a changed position, both symbolic and actual, in which he or she can concretely sense and recognize a difference in perspective and self-perception. Students may not be or actually believe at that point in their movement that they are successful, but the movement can serve as a springboard toward that learning, knowing, and being goal.

This movement is key when concerns about "teachability" arise. Too many schools, their administrators and, ultimately, teachers give up on students like Maria and Ruben. Teachers may still physically have them in their classrooms, but they do not engage them in a community that practices that which is required to be, or learn to be, successful students. When students like Maria and Ruben get to such communities, often they are already behind most others in the classroom academically. Most teachers know that it is difficult to bring such students up to grade level. It is seen as extra work. Or teachers simply may not know what to do with such students. The teachers then blame the teachers before them. Or the students' parents. Or their poverty. Or the students themselves. The students are seen as a burden, with too many deficits. They rarely are seen as individuals with potential. Or teachers may not know *how* to see these students as individuals with potential. Although the CAMP students in this study were impacted by a number of social, economic, cultural, educational, linguistic, and personal complexities, they thrived when they were able to inhabit and enact their potential in their first year of college.

Ultimately, Maria and Ruben still had hope and the desire for an education, as did Laura, Cristina, and Luz. That's where the possibilities in programs like CAMP and the communities of practice that they create can give some hope to the marginalized and their teachers. It is only if and when schools and teachers of the marginalized understand how they can tap into this hope for the marginalized that they will see more student engagement in schools. There will be more learning. Fewer dropouts. Even better test scores. But the pedagogical approaches of the vast majority of schools today are coming up short. Some readers may think that because this study took place at a community college there are no implications for K–12 education. But the concept of a community of practice is applicable for all grade levels (to be discussed below), because the ingredients are mostly intangible until they are enacted—resilience, desire, love, hope. Our schools have indeed lost sight of the power of these intangibles in the teaching of our marginalized. But in these intangibles can come results in teaching and learning.

So what is possible in this pursuit to improve schooling for the marginalized? Where can hope lead us in this pursuit? Freire (2004) argued that we cannot just simply hope. Change, reform, empowerment, and improvement in the educational system for the marginalized must also be accompanied by ideas, concrete plans, and practice. That is how we might realize the possible. And so we return to the illustration of Ruben and Maria feeling successful based on their own terms and realizations. Although they did not successfully complete

CAMP and the first year of college, they realized a new sense of what they were able to accomplish in college within the broader picture of the complexities of their lives. They learned what was possible for *them*. And this happens to many marginalized and minoritized groups within US educational institutions. Students are at the brink of realizing an empowered sense of self in the trajectory toward learning to be a successful student, but somehow we fail to capitalize on this place in their learning. Our current schooling paradigm is designed not to recognize that movement, learning, and understanding toward a successful student identity. For example, No Child Left Behind policies consistently label schools with high numbers of English learners as failing, despite the great achievements and progress such students make in an academic year learning social and academic language. As educators, administrators, and policy makers, we must do something with these new student understandings and sense of success in a pragmatic and empowering way. We cannot let students like Ruben and Maria languish in their momentary feeling of success, knowing that this will soon fade. Or, as with the English learners, allow others to label them as failures. Although such an emotion in the realization of knowing they can do college or learn English may successfully carry them into another community of practice, we cannot risk the chance of a sense of empowerment and possibility to fade. So what can we do for students like Ruben and Maria? And how can we build on these new understandings derived from what we learned from the CAMP student experience? In the following sections, I explore various issues that emerged from the findings and discuss the implications and recommendations that can be drawn from this study for all levels of schooling.

## Different Measures of Success: The Cases of Maria and Ruben

The CAMP program design and the people involved presented particular guidelines and expectations of "success" to the students, but some students were not able to fulfill such obligations. Maria, for example, left the program early because the complexities of her life situation made it difficult to handle the logistics of attending college and succeeding academically. Ruben was not able to meet the minimum 2.0 GPA requirement, frequently exhibiting practices that prevented him from being academically successful. However, although students like Maria and Ruben may not have "succeeded" according to either the typical, mainstream standards of success or in terms of the goals of the CAMP program, they understood the *necessity* of learning how to balance multiple identities within multiple communities of practice. It was within their own time continuum and frame of reference, however, that they defined their notion of success. Their experiences in the program and in their first year of college were an initial step in their trajectories toward their own unique goals and definitions of success. Their gaining entry into college through CAMP was the beginning of their own learning of their individually distinct processes of arriving at successful student identities.

Ruben was allowed to engage in a practice that required immersion and investment in a new way of being and becoming—learning to be a successful student—that differed from his past practices in schooling. Ruben explained that he saw his physical and emotional presence as a successful act because it went beyond his own expectations of being a student. He felt successful because he was given entry into the college world, through the CAMP scholarship, and he felt that he was involved enough to have learned from his mistakes and successes. There were moments where he exhibited successful academic practices, such as in his writing. Ruben also noted that his success was defined by his new ability to be a part of a community like CAMP and to learn from those involved. He discovered he was able to thrive in a new community of practice in a school, something he struggled to do in past schooling. The agency required to reach this point of self-defined success was influenced by the supportive network of invested others in the CAMP program experience.

Maria saw herself as successful because she discovered that she indeed could practice that which was required to be a successful student. She knew she could be a college student. Considering her tremendous responsibilities as a young mother of two children, Maria was successful because she enacted her aspirations. Contrary to a popular discourse that stigmatizes teen mothers, Maria illustrated resilience and feelings of empowerment to continue her education. Reflecting what Zachry (2005) found in her study of teenage mothers, being in school was a significant experience for Maria and was a tool for advancing her educational and professional aspirations. Maria initially was fortunate to have the logistical support and child-care services of her mother, but that eventually was not available. With her financial situation, she could not afford child care for her two sons while she attended school. So she had to withdraw from the CAMP program; it was an emotional time for Maria that made her feel extremely disappointed in herself. Briefly, she felt like a failure. But, after some time to reflect, Maria realized that she was successful because she committed to the program. She knew she was successful because she not only showed up but was actively engaged. She knew she was successful because she made good grades. It was not her choice to quit college and CAMP. Forces outside of Maria made that choice for her.

Educators and policy makers must look more closely at how they are defining success for our marginalized students, and the impact this definition has on student presence, efforts, and progress in schools. Although educators must be careful to continue to challenge students at all levels and maintain high expectations, especially for culturally and linguistically diverse students, they must recognize that schooling success is relative to time, situations, and access. Mexican-descent students coming from marginalized backgrounds may not have had the positive experiences or access to collaborative communities of practice that would engage them in the practice of becoming successful students. These opportunities sometimes come very late in their schooling, or they may never come at all.

In today's schools, positive educational experiences for marginalized students like Ruben and Maria are rare. Gang-affiliated students may not show up to class. They may be feared, or teachers will not want to give them a chance, because, to them, they are invisible in the larger setting of high school (Conchas, 2001). Teen mothers are often vilified and stigmatized (Wilson and Huntington, 2006). As a result, we see pervasive disengagement in school and habitual failure. Schools do not know how to effectively work with such student populations, so situationally marginalized and struggling students are allowed to "fall through the cracks." The social and economic consequences are severe, and for all. Teen mothers are less likely to complete high school and go to college than are those who delay having children until at least the age of 20 (Hoffman, 2006). And gang membership is often a life of violence and crime (Vigil, 2003), far removed from the benefits of an education. So it is important for educators to understand that when such marginalized student populations experience a type of success similar to what Ruben and Maria experienced, they must recognize such success and build on it to keep students engaged and continuing to learn, allowing that feeling to become the foundation for learning the identity of a successful student.

## Creating a Place for the Possible

### A Chance to Learn about Self, Life, and Possibilities

Education for marginalized students requires that they have entry into a community of practice for learning, whether that be in a one-on-one interaction and/or relationship with an educator, or as part of a community in a classroom that engages in collaborative practices of learning. The CAMP scholarship concretely and symbolically provided access to a place of opportunity for the students in this study, which Lave and Wenger (1991) argue is paramount to the process of learning in a community of practice. The CAMP students were given access to a community of learners, as well as to more knowledgeable others who were guiding/teaching/ modeling/apprenticing the students to be and become successful students and contribute to their learning of a successful student identity. Students were given access to a new social, cultural, and educational paradigm that provided a new understanding of what schooling could be.

Schools, classrooms, and individual educators can give students access to communities of practice where collaboration and effective teaching and learning are occurring. In that community, the student is interacting in ways with the teachers and others that contribute to a positive sense of self, as well as to the other elements of a successful student identity. This often involves educators creating schools, classrooms, and even small, diversified groups within classrooms that are grounded in high expectations for teaching and learning. This pedagogy is approached with a firm, humanizing understanding of the histories, cultures, languages, and unique needs of students, especially the marginalized. And in this coupling of high expectations and humanizing pedagogy (Bartolomé, 1994) that is practiced by all, community will often organically emerge through negotiations, tensions, struggles, and successes. But first students must have entry into this community of practice.

## Creating Communities of Practice

Student marginalization outside of school is powerful, and can easily thwart trajectories toward being or becoming successful students. This can result in further marginalization in schools where there is already segregation and isolation from mainstream communities and contexts (Orfield and Lee, 2005). These locations are not conducive to teaching-learning dynamics that provide opportunities to learn what is required of successful students. As a result, the marginalized are seeing themselves less and less in the various aspects of school because of our current schooling structure (Koyama and Gibson, 2007) and the new paradigm of high stakes and standardization. So students disengage. For these students, success begins not with academics, but with entry into a community of practice that accepts and embraces who they are and recognizes the need to apprentice them to the ultimate goals of good grades, the honor roll, independent learning, critical thinking, lifelong learning, and empowerment. Learning in these communities means much more than what schools today define as learning. As I mentioned earlier and argue here, learning is engagement. Engagement is identity. And identity is the foundation for academic success.

According to Wenger (1998), "in spite of curriculum, discipline, and exhortation, the learning that is most personally transformative turns out to be the learning that involves membership in these communities of practice" (p. 6). In the past, segregation for Mexican Americans was intentional, blatant, systemic, and physical. Today, many marginalized Mexican Americans are no longer members of communities in our schools and classrooms who practice any sense of learning that transforms or empowers. They exist apart from or on the margins in such communities, lumbering along in their schooling, and simply look on as others succeed. It is a system that continues to privilege only a few who are members of these communities of practice. For the marginalized, the current design and teaching-learning dynamics of high-stakes, numbers-driven schools function as sociopsychologically and socioculturally segregating mechanisms that undermine what learning is and/or can be. That is, too many marginalized Mexican Americans are only physically present in the classroom. They are simply there. But membership in a community of practice is only the beginning. In these communities, the interactions that occur must also contribute to a positive trajectory toward the development of a successful student identity.

According to Wenger (1998), you cannot design communities of practice and the learning that occurs within them. However, such communities can be designed *for* this type of learning to naturally occur. There is no specific model that engages students in a trajectory of being and becoming successful as individuals and as students. Wenger (1998) presents ideas on how the design of a community of practice has implications in education, while other scholars (Barton and Tusting, 2005) present studies that illustrate iterations of communities of practices in various contexts (e.g., business, the political, adult education, etc). For those who desire to implement change, the concept of community of practice is appealing, because "a seemingly natural formation which enhances learning can be consciously developed" (Barton and Tusting, 2005, p. 3). Consciously planned and designed, the groundwork for the CAMP community of practice was inherent in the scholarship providing access, the roles of members, support services, and the standard college curriculum. The community of practice toward the learning of a successful student identity was begun even before the students arrived. But this preteaching and prelearning are not just skills, knowledge, or even understanding for the marginalized to learn, acquire, or practice. The teaching–learning dynamic that occurs in a community of practice is a way of being that is unrealized; and not present until it is ready to be present.

The concept of communities of practice in education is a constantly evolving, dynamic, and extensive web of microcommunities and key interactions within a larger community of practice. Lave and Wenger (1991) more closely explored learning that occurs in informal settings, while Wenger (1998) later presented how communities of practice can work within educational institutions. In higher education there has been a call to learn more about how the concept of communities of practice can guide educators and administrators to help us better understand student learning. According to Lea (2005) it can help us see how institutional practices continue to exclude the marginalized and "lay bare some of the differential ways in which meanings are both contested and constituted for participants in the processes of teaching and learning, [for] both students and tutors" (p. 194). Based on the findings of this study, a community of practice and the learning that occurs therein happen within an overlap of both formal and informal pedagogical settings, interactions, and relationships. The communities are between a teacher and a student, between peers within a small group, among students within the classroom, and/or within an entire school. For the marginalized student, formal and informal pedagogy are one and the same, because they both have significant meaning in their learning.

Communities of practice are based on a philosophy and design that involves creating opportunities to engage in desired ways of being. That practice will differ for educators and students according to needs and goals. For example, one class may engage in the practice of learning chemistry and getting good at it, while another may engage in the practice of learning how to do well on standardized tests. Practice is a way of being in the world that is not final or fixed; rather, it is a process of becoming other desired ways of being and knowing. This especially can have major implications for marginalized students. Their marginalization has kept them from participating in a community of practice that supports their trajectory and desire in learning to become successful students. But if effective and responsive educators have recognized their marginalization by knowing the students' family, community, and past schooling experiences, it is never too late to participate in a community of practice that promotes and engages in the learning of successful student identities.

## Learning Together

The learning communities curriculum was unique to this CAMP program and was meant for the students to experience particular coursework as a cohort. The learning communities were restricted to the first two quarters of the academic year to provide the students a chance to utilize one another as resources on both personal and academic levels. The last quarter was designed to be a time for students to explore the dynamics of other courses with students outside of the CAMP community, so they could begin to learn to be more independent of the CAMP cohort. Because the learning communities curriculum allowed the students to complete assignments that functioned to meet the objectives of both courses, it was an opportunity for them not only to effectively and efficiently complete course requirements but to gel as a cohort and a type of family in navigating the academic world. The students in this study found the learning communities valuable, because they engaged in academic efforts and struggles with students like themselves and felt comfortable and confident in their interactions and involvement in classes. They felt they were in a supportive environment in the learning communities and could depend on others to help them meet social, personal, and academic needs throughout each academic quarter.

## Invested Others

"Invested others" in this study refers to the notion that individual human resources within a social and academic network can contribute in their own unique way to the agency and empowerment of students learning to be and become. This study found that ethnicity and life experience functioned in unique ways for the students in terms of the type of knowledge that was being passed or co-constructed. Students who had similar experiences and backgrounds with invested others created a bridge of commonality and community in a sociocultural and sociohistorical discourse of struggle, being, and becoming in identity. Even if the invested other and the student were not similar in ethnicity or background, another common element emerged in the form of willingness to give and receive in communication on a landscape of academic skills, knowledge, and empowerment grounded in motivation, from both parties. Building on Lave and Wenger's (1991) idea of legitimate peripheral participation, this dynamic gave legitimacy to the CAMP students by affirming their history, presence, and struggles as they practiced from the periphery. But even within these understandings based on commonalities, the invested others ultimately offered different perspectives. According to Wenger (1998), a community of practice must be a place that allows for transformation to occur, letting identities absorb these new perspectives in order to make them a part of the newly forming identities. When imagination is aligned with these new perspectives, he says, it "produces the ability to act with respect to a broad and rich picture of the world" (p. 218). The interactions that CAMP students had with the invested others presented new ways of seeing the world that they could be a part of, which they ultimately internalized.

For K–12 schooling, invested others are those who first approach the education of their students, especially marginalized students of color, with the idea to empower and create change for the student. An invested other exists in all segments of the social and academic networks of a student schooling experience, ready to contribute to the advancement and learning of students when it is needed. It is a way of thinking and preparation for an educator ready to provide guidance/assistance/teaching and apprenticeship toward the target learning experience that is the goal of a particular community of practice of learning, empowerment, and success.

## Key Interactions and Their Importance for Marginalized Students

In school reform efforts, the intricate matters are sometimes the ones that get overlooked in trying to determine what contributes to students' success in school. Building on the idea that micro-interactions are significant in schooling, key interactions in social educational settings are those that significantly matter to situationally marginalized Mexican American students. Many of the marginalized attend schools where poverty is prevalent, students are disengaged, opportunity is limited, and teachers and parents struggle to understand how to get such students motivated to learn, care, and succeed. An understanding of the power of key interactions is a pedagogical tool that can address these issues. In the micro-interactions between people, there are words and ideas that sometimes trigger profound understanding and insight and lead to some sense of transformation.

It is essential for educators at all levels of schooling to recognize the power in creating situations in which key interactions can occur between them and their students who are being recognized.

By understanding the use and pedagogical dynamic of key interactions within a community of practice, teachers can still be effective and empowering without the concern of the time needed to establish profound relationships with students. Key interactions that are positive and empowering would go a long way in bridging the gaps that often exist between educators and their students.

As the findings of this study illustrate, key interactions are those that occur between student and educators, or members of the community, and contribute a sense of agency, knowledge, and/or empowerment to the student. For example, key interactions may emerge from a brief compliment, a dialogue on the improvement of academic work, or words of encouragement in the hallway. Such an interaction may be the impetus for students to perform better academically, to decide not to ditch class for the day, and/or to realize their potential in school, a sport, or an activity they previously did not have the courage to do. Key interactions do not have to be relationships with students. They can be the strategic use of additive and positive discourse, words, and ways of being with the students that create a moment of understanding, learning, development, collaboration, and ultimately empowerment. Additive discourses seen through key interactions may result in additive schooling, as opposed to subtractive schooling (Valenzuela, 1999). These discourses allow students who have been marginalized to internalize a new discourse that includes their language, culture, and identities as part of broader everyday interactions, pedagogy, and learning in the interactions they have with others.

A key interaction is also the recognition of something good, or potentially good, about the student. It involves the teacher acting upon that knowledge by interacting with the student in a way that reflects the need *to recognize*. That is, someone who is in a position of power or authority, or someone whom a student admires or respects, acknowledges that a student may be living in or has come from a marginalized or stigmatized place in society. They then commit to presenting a sense of what is possible for the student, rooted in the knowledge of the student's background. This was seen, for example, in Ruben's English instructor, William, allowing him to write about his past and life experiences. Others, such as CAMP staff member Israel and the community member Lalo Delgado, may utilize a common understanding of struggle, hard work, effort, and ultimately success as a target for the students to reach. Additionally, ethnicity, race, language, and life hardship may also be utilized as a common discourse between student and that person of authority. The student then builds upon that understanding as a point of departure for learning and uses those words of encouragement, wisdom, and such as fuel for his or her agency and potential in accomplishing a particular goal. Key interactions are moments that allow students to gain a deeper sense of self and understanding in their roles as students. This occurs in that immediate reaction to the internalized discourse that fed that sense of self or possible self.

In today's schooling paradigm that emphasizes learning based on single-test results, we have lost a basic understanding of the human aspect of teaching and learning. We have failed to realize the power in the relationship between student and teacher. We have forgotten that the teacher–student relationship (not specific teaching methods, approaches, or curricula) is the first and most important aspect of effective teaching and learning for our marginalized students (Bartolomé, 1994; Gibson, 2005; M. Reyes, 1992). In our pursuit of exemplary schools, we have lost sight of how the teacher–student collaborative relationship can empower the social and economically marginalized to be resilient and to embrace hope, and can provide opportunity to be successful in school and beyond (Cummins, 1996). These relationships promote students' academic achievement. They are not just ways to have students feel good about themselves. They are much more.

Few schools today practice or have institutionalized community building, collaboration, and positive interactions in the teaching and learning process. We often hear that such efforts are too time-consuming. They are stressful. It is difficult to manage classrooms in this way. There is no control. The students cheat. They don't care. They don't learn anyway. Trueba (1989) believed that the absence of communities with effective teaching–learning contexts and interactions indicates a failure of the school system to provide learners with the necessary opportunities to engage in social interactions that lead to learning. Key interactions are a reflection and a result of collaborative relationships and understandings between student and teacher. Furthering our understanding of the micro-level dynamics of pedagogy such as key interactions in communities of practice provides insight into how teachers might better integrate such a philosophy in their teaching, hopefully without feeling burdened.

## Program Logistics

The CAMP program was an invaluable resource and "ticket" for the students to have access to a college experience with support and resources to aid in their becoming successful students. But logistical details emerged from this study that presented a number of problems for the students involved that many of the socioeconomically and academically privileged may not even think about. First, because many of the students were academically underprepared, they had to take a number of developmental courses (course numbers listed at or below 090), for which they could not earn college-level credit. Although it is sensible to provide courses appropriate for individual student readiness and levels, the problem inherent in this practice is that the students are taking coursework that does not earn them credit toward a college degree. Additionally, since CAMP is only a one-year program, time and money are essential for the students. Taking developmental courses takes away resources in "doing college" and working toward a college degree. And, although this may seem like a postsecondary issue, the need for developmental courses at the college level presents many troubling questions about the ability of the K–12 system to adequately prepare marginalized students for college-level coursework.

In an immediate and concrete manner, one way to remedy the issue of developmental coursework would be to provide additional funding for students who have made good progress in their first year in the form of a scholarship. For example, a two-year scholarship would keep students from having to disrupt their trajectory after the successful completion of their first year and would provide critical financial resources. Additionally, because many of the students that go into CAMP come from educationally marginalized situations, students could take developmental courses in the summer *before* they begin taking college-level coursework, paid for by the scholarship. The developmental courses the students take could be taken principally in math and English, subjects with which all the CAMP students struggled in this study, and taken intensively five days a week in a two- to four-week time frame.

Attention would also be given to preparing students to take the Accuplacer computer placement test to ensure they achieved at least the minimum score required to enter college-level courses. The minimum was recently raised to an 80 at Next Step Community College, ten points more than the minimum score of 70 originally mandated. This new score requirement on the Accuplacer could potentially have devastating effects on students like those entering CAMP, because the majority of the students struggled to score that 70.

Although students like Maria expressed a desire to attend college and exhibited great effort and agency, Maria's responsibilities as a parent were too much for her to continue on in the balance between life and school. Maria's child-care issues created problematic and conflicting situations for her and eventually forced her to prematurely leave the program. To better serve students with multiple obligations such as the kind Maria had, even programs like CAMP must be redesigned. A CAMP program, for example, can provide child-care facilities or at least provide the funding to perhaps pay other CAMP students who need part-time work to help care for the children of other students in the program. This could be one way to alleviate some of the logistical issues that prevent some students from attending and completing a postsecondary education.

One of the barriers to this idea is funding. CAMP is currently only a one-year scholarship program that is completely federally funded, which, depending on the politics du jour, could be reduced or eliminated.


## Tensions in Gender Roles, Romance, and Aspirations: The Case of Luz

We must pay attention to the educational experiences of Latinas like Laura, Cristina, Luz, and Maria, who now outnumber Latino males in college and constitute the largest ethnic minority group of women in the United States (González, Jovel, and Stoner, 2004). Studies that examine the schooling experiences of Latinas have revealed that there are gendered patterns in what they do to create opportunities for success in college (Barajas and Pierce, 2001). That is, Latinas engage in particular strategies different from those of Latinos in pathways to and while in college to ensure their personal and academic well-being. As Latinas, they must also contend with different social, cultural, familial, and peer pressures of being a woman living in today's society (Anzaldúa, 1999). Latina roles and identities are often pulled in different directions by those who are trying to define those roles and identities for them. So complexities and tensions arise from their relationships with others—their parents, relatives, friends, and lovers. This was especially the case for Luz.

Some young women of Mexican descent living in the United States, such as Luz, whether recent immigrants or second- or third-generation, often experience a life of clashing multiple identities rooted in ambivalence about the expectations of being a woman. They may come from a traditional Mexican value system, but at the same time are prodded by American ideals of assimilation for academic, personal, and professional success. Luz is an example of a young Latina caught in a tension of competing discourses. She feared that romance leading to marriage and domesticity would subvert her aspirations of educational and career success. She did not think the two could coexist. And the lack of support for her ambitions from geographically distant, but still influential, relatives in Mexico somehow filtered into her consciousness and identity/ies. That lack of support from relatives came in the form of fatalistic taunts about marriage, motherhood, and domesticity. Although she resisted by continuing her education and doing well academically, she was still moved by this discourse.

For many Mexican American women, "to *ser mujer* entails negotiating dichotomies defining gender and sexuality that continue to persist in the home space" (Villenas and Moreno, 2001, p. 678). Perhaps Luz's extended family saw her desire to go to college conflict with their expectation of Luz to eventually carry out her roles that reflect *marianismo,* a cultural value in which many Latino families see woman as self-sacrificing family caretaker (Sy, 2006). The world of the Mexican immigrant families that Valdés (1996) studied was one "in which relationships and human ties were far more important than options or choices" (p. 171). Maybe Luz's distant family saw her desire for college as a gesture toward the devaluation of, and further distancing of herself in, her relationship with them.

This tension is often part of the stresses of families, especially for the parents of Latinas, dealing with the inevitable transition from a complete commitment to a family-based Mexican value system to an American-based value system based on individuality, personal persistence, and devotion to academics and a career. Part of this transition is the physical moving from home to college, for which many parents, although supportive of their daughters' educational pursuits, are not prepared (González, Jovel, and Stoner, 2004).

But why did Luz struggle so much with the unsupportive words of her relatives? Why did she fear "falling in love so easily," as she wrote in her letter to self? Her struggles and fears may have emanated from a tension of old and newly forming identities in a contentious patriarchal society. Or perhaps the immediate realities of the lives of her sisters were constant reminders of what she saw as inevitable domesticity if she were to marry. In this society, the expectations that still exist for the roles of women ignite identity and gender-role conflicts for such women, who have to function between and within other cultural spaces (Schutte, 1993), as well as battle discourses that contradict their own. Anzaldúa (1999) calls this juxtaposition of cultures and worlds the formation of an identity—the new mestiza—and argues for a more complex portrayal of Chicanas' lives. She finds that

> cradled in one culture, sandwiched between two cultures, straddling all three cultures and their value systems, la mestiza undergoes a struggle of flesh, struggle of borders, an inner war. Like all people, we perceive the version of reality that our culture communicates. Like others having or living in more than one culture, we get multiple, often opposing messages. The coming together of two self-consistent but habitually incompatible frames of reference causes *un choque,* a cultural collision (p. 100).

This complexity often involves dealing with the pressures to maintain the call to be one type of woman, while the call of the new mestiza urges Chicanas to fulfill a desire to be something different and more.

Perhaps the words and discourse from Luz's relatives intermingled with the broader discourse of the idealized notions of love and romance that often dominate not just the lives of Latinas, but also the lives of so many young girls today. What is often typical for young Chicanas in the formation of new identities are the experiences that represent the continued journey between the old self and the new mestiza influenced by a culture of romance and leading to potential domestication. Pat Mora (1993) admits in the efforts to push Latinas to achieve academically and be self-empowered, the romantic ideal is what often dominates the desires and values of young Chicana women. She suggests,

> We can appeal to young women's minds with our facts and sta-tistics, but who is daily tugging at their hearts, at our hearts? Who keeps teaching heterosexual women to hum, "Some day my prince will come"? Most novels, magazines, movies, the "soaps" or novellas, the talk shows focus women's attention on the primacy of a snuggly relationship with a man. Deep in their most private selves, do young women wait for their male solu-tion, ashamed to admit this aloud, sparing themselves our cold frowns, the frowns of mothers, aunts, professors? They know what we want to hear, know all the right phrases and reasons— self-determination, self-interest, self-direction—but is their un-speakable truth that without *the* man at their side they just don't like themselves? (p. 63)

When presented with new life choices and the consequences of pulled identities, it is a reflection of a Chicana's ability to cope "by developing a tolerance for ambiguity. . . . She has a plural personal-ity, she operates in a pluralistic mode—nothing is thrust out, the good the bad and the ugly, nothing rejected, nothing abandoned. Not only does she sustain contradictions, she turns the ambiva-lence into something else" (Anzaldúa, 1999, p. 101). Luz exemplified Anzaldúa's sentiments here—she still continued on her educational trajectory but seemingly wrestled with romance constantly. She re-sisted advances in courtship but merely tolerated the reality that this is how it will always be. This is a common site of tension and a pro-cess that involves new choices for a woman in a new postmodern world that may be distinct from their old world of gender roles, identity, and the structure of the traditional family (Hirsch, 2003; Winn, 2006).

Gaining an intimate look at the schooling experiences and personal struggles of Latinas like Luz should provide educators insight to the pressures of romance, resilience, and strategic coping. Because students like Luz must deal with the process of functioning, surviving, and succeeding in multiple communities of practice, social networks of support and understanding are paramount in providing the agency and empowerment that will fuel their efforts to better navigate communities such as college. We know that Latinas value the humanizing aspect of interactions within these networks, and it is often needed to be academically successful. Family support contributes to the academic achievement of Latinas in college (Sy, 2006), which reflects how important relationships are for them in their path to school success (Barajas and Pierce, 2001). Similarly, when Latinas are making decisions about college and how to get there, they seek out similar support and relationships in school agents (Zarate and Gallimore, 2005).

Gender roles and expectations are still so entrenched in society that we must continue to be cognizant of what parts these dynamics might play in forcing young women like Luz to believe that choosing one life track is done at the expense of denying another. Of course, we know this is not true. Women juggle multiple identities in multiple communities of practice daily. And Luz is an example of resisting this either/or dichotomy and reconciling competing discourses. She exemplifies the power of choice and empowerment in effectively dealing with unsupportive relatives and the fear of a relationship leading to a life of domesticity. Her experience also reminds us that Latinas deal with adversity in unique ways, reflecting high levels of self-efficacy and strategizing out of necessity to be successful in college (Zell, 2010). Luz followed her pathway according to her goals, her desires, her plan.

## Taking Risks and the Emergence of Voice and Identity: The Peculiar Problem of "Shyness" for Latinas in School

All of the women in this study revealed that they were "shy" to some extent. They admitted that they often struggled with expressing themselves in front of large groups or in class. Being shy was being quiet, having a soft voice. From a cultural perspective, for many

Hispanic children, to be quiet is to be respectful and often results from a socialization process that is grounded in cultural expectations of behavior (Leyendecker, Harwood, Lamb, and Schölmerich, 2002). Such behavior is often interpreted as shyness in children. It is common for many people to admit to being shy, as the CAMP women did. But is it just a personality trait? Gudiño and Lau (2010) found that shyness may be a culturally specific socialization process through parent-guided behaviors that promote harmony and connectedness with adults and other children. They also discussed how shyness may be context-specific. They found that children felt more anxiety when shy with their peers than with adults. Overall, they found that the level of shyness in the Hispanic children in their study was relative to the extent to which Hispanic youth adopted US cultural values, attitudes, and behaviors. The more acculturated children were less shy than those who were less acculturated.

But, as adults, why were the CAMP women so shy and quiet? What else can their shyness mean? The common finding between all the CAMP women in this study expressing how shyness was a factor in their past development as successful students prompts further discussion and exploration beyond this study. In many ways, the inability of these Latinas to be more open, expressive, and outgoing in their interactions with teachers and others prevented them from discovering more of their personal and academic capabilities. Were Laura, Cristina, Luz, and Maria also shy as children? If so, could their shyness from childhood have carried over into adulthood and become an impeding variable in the use and development of their voice, preventing them from reaching their full academic potential? In this sense, voice is both an actual and a symbolic voice of the CAMP students that serves as a tool and a mechanism for active participation. This voice allows them to be heard and understood. This voice "defines them as social beings" (Darder, 1991, p. 66). So, because shyness can be seen as a muted form of expression, the messages and content in a shy Latina's voice are often diluted. And in the context of schools voice is essential to the "student's ability to participate and enter into dialogue within the classroom, and as a result, participate in a democratic social process" (p. 66).

Their shyness may have been a shell that protected them from the many unknown elements that come with social interactions; but it was also a barrier to knowing their true voice and thus their true identity. For Laura, her shyness potentially led to a misunderstanding by others of her as a student. She felt isolated and withdrawn from the schooling process. Cristina, Luz, and Maria talked about how their shyness kept them from participating in class or expressing their thoughts and opinions before entering CAMP, and even in the early days of being in the program. Their shyness prevented them from developing their voices.

As Cristina, Laura, Luz, and Maria revealed, their participation in the Adventure Learning course and their participation in some classes showed how they could be another "self" through the use and development of their voices. They discovered that the social context and activities in places like the Adventure Learning classes were designed to encourage engagement and interaction among students. Opportunities were created for the students to enact a new sense of self and possible self. Dialogue, problem-solving games, and sharing of emotional and moving tales of their personal and schooling histories created a space for expressing empathy and the building of community. The once-shy girls realized that the expression of ideas, feelings, and knowledge was empowering and contributed to the development of voice that energized their trajectory toward learning to be a successful student and woman. Laura, Cristina, Luz, and Maria understood the power of taking risks in learning and becoming. Taking risks is necessary in searching for possible selves in the identities of successful students.

## The Weight of Academic Marginalization

Schools today are still struggling to adequately prepare students academically (Greene and Forster, 2003; McCarthy and Kuh, 2006) and provide them the necessary information to feel ready for entering and managing college (Kirst and Venezia, 2001). For Hispanic students, of the 52 percent that graduate from high school, only 16 percent are college-ready (Greene and Forster, 2003). Because the students in this study had to take remedial courses in math and English, their present experiences reflected a history of academic marginalization and lack of academic preparation. Students like Cristina were frustrated with the coursework in high school and surprised by how difficult the English courses were in college. For others, like Luz, in spite of her determination and good grades in high school, she was still relegated to some remediation in her first quarter of college. Her academic experiences in high school did not leave her well prepared for work at the community-college level.

College readiness is an enduring problem for many students. But for the less privileged, minoritized, and marginalized students, being ready for college has serious implications for completing college in a timely manner, if ever (Greene and Forster, 2003). Because there are so many students who are not prepared for college today, this epidemic does not just reflect issues of individual determination, parent support, or even the effects of socioeconomic status, race, and ethnicity. Although these factors indeed impact some students, when the numbers show that nationwide so many students are not ready for college, we must look elsewhere to understand its complexity.

The K–12 system apparently is not doing an adequate job of preparing students to do college (Greene and Forster, 2003). For the marginalized, this problem with the system of schooling on which they rely to give them a chance to change their life situations makes their chances for success even grimmer. Yet the CAMP students highlighted here showed resilience in the face of the weight of their academic marginalization. And although this resilience cannot be discounted, we cannot depend on the resilience of thousands of individual students to compensate for the failures of an entire schooling system. A history of academic marginalization and its impact on school-going efforts is a serious problem, and we must continue to carefully study, scrutinize, and reform that system that is creating this problem. We still have much work to do in our K–12 system in preparing our students to be college-ready.

## Seeing Potential

Most, if not all, of the CAMP students presented in this study would not be considered "college material" according to the standardized way of seeing how students are prepared for college. But the majority of the students in this study successfully navigated what was required to make their way through their first year of college, in spite of their marginalization going into the CAMP program. Perhaps they represent what Trueba (2002) realized about children of immigrants and marginalized minority student populations. He saw such students as having evolving abilities to adapt and enact a new cultural capital and ways of being, surviving, and even thriving in multiple contexts. In their learning, the CAMP students evolved and thrived. The CAMP students and what they learned, realized, and accomplished illustrates how the marginalized cannot be forgotten.

Consider that Luz was the only student from among those studied who took AP courses, something typically done by those intending to go to college, and was encouraged by teachers in high school to pursue college. The other students involved did not have the same exposure to supportive environments and human resources to fuel a desire or at least plant the thought of the possibility of pursuing higher education. But, for a long time, Luz still struggled with the idea that she could be a successful college student, even after she enrolled in college through CAMP. Luz needed more time and support in forging the empowered components of her new identity/ies. She needed other discourses of possibility to reconcile with the unsupportive discourses imposing other ways of being she was not ready for at that point in her life. Part of recognizing potential in students is understanding what they are struggling with in their identities that prevent them from seeing their own potential.

Schools need to look more closely at who and what is defining "college material" in culturally and linguistically diverse students, especially those coming from marginalized backgrounds. Aggressive efforts must be taken to create schooling and classroom environments that see the potential for *all* students to pursue and do well in higher education. This involves culturally responsive teaching (Gay, 2000) and an empowering education that instills a spirit of hope and possibility (Darder, 1991) in the student by integrating his or her schooling and personal histories into teaching approaches.

Consider Cristina's experience. I often wonder what would have happened had Cristina been tracked into higher-level, more challenging coursework in high school. Where would she be? Would she have received other scholarship opportunities? How would her self-perception have changed? In today's high-stakes, standardized schooling paradigm, our school systems are not set up in a way that allows for teachers to recognize the potential in students like Cristina. Sadly, too many students of Mexican descent like Cristina continue to fall through the cracks of our educational system. Cristina was fortunate enough to receive the CAMP scholarship, a financial and confidence springboard to success for someone like her.

Cristina's is one story of success. So many similar stories are untold, but we know they exist. The teachers who work with these students and work hard to keep them from being marginalized or being failed by the system know these stories all too well. But they cannot "save" all students, again because of the way our current school system is set up—little teacher support, meaningless professional development, top-down mandates to "teach to the test," and working in schools that are simply too big, and where students like Cristina just get lost while their potential is not realized. What can we learn from these stories? Cristina's story is continuing proof that students like her can succeed once given the opportunity and a support system, such as the CAMP program. But they can also succeed *despite* the lack of support and educational opportunity provided in high school before entering college. Indeed, they get through high school.

We know that there is still a lot of work that needs to be done with our school systems and how they are designed to meet the needs (or not) of other marginalized Mexican-descent student groups, such as immigrants, migrants, and English learners. But we also learned that on a micro level, our educators need to be given the tools, resources, and time to find more students like Cristina in their classrooms, so they won't have to wait for a CAMP scholarship to catch them before they fall further through the cracks. On a broader policy level of education, that is why we should care about the CAMP student experience. Although it shows us that students like Cristina, Luz, Laura, Maria, and Ruben can be brought from the margins of school and society to thrive in college, schools should not allow students like them to become so entrenched in their marginalization. Schools must create access to and opportunities within communities of practice similar to what was done in CAMP, much sooner in the schooling experiences of, not only the marginalized, but all students. We know that today schools are struggling to make teaching and learning meaningful. The conceptual construct of communities of practice should be examined more closely to see how it can translate to an effective pedagogical approach in their schools. Such communities may help teachers to better understand and know their students, their experiences, and their stories. And then maybe students will realize meaning in their learning bridged by this connection to their teachers.

Seeing all students, but especially the marginalized, as "college material" is part of a pedagogy of investment of confidence in students. This is especially so for students who may not have had the opportunity to interact with educators or engage in learning communities in their past schooling that could contribute to their agency, sense of hope, and the reality of college. But too many continue to define students as "college material" by their participation in a college-track curriculum, high SAT/ACT scores, or stellar grades. Gándara (1999) argues that "we have reason to worry that a great deal of potential may be squandered because of adherence to a point system that gives no value to diversity and fails to acknowledge significant differences in opportunities to learn" (p. 185). The characteristics of possibility are found not only in academic performance, grades, or points, but also in the stories students tell to their teachers, of what makes them cry, what burdens them, and what drives them to want to do better. Perhaps we may recognize better how a student can be "college material" through their stories. And we may see how the potential may have been there all along.

## Final Thoughts: Deriving the Simple from the Complex

Simple. No one ever uses this word to describe how schools work, how curriculum is created, how teachers teach, how students learn. Schooling and the process of educating the masses will never be simple. Yet, when you look closely at the CAMP program design, there is a hint of simplicity in it. At the core of this simplicity is a dynamic of relationships and interactions that occur within the CAMP community of practice. Indeed, the human aspect of teaching and learning drove persistence, resilience, and academic success in the CAMP students. As Bartolomé (1994) aptly argued some time ago, it is the humanizing aspect of teaching and learning that we often ignore in our pedagogy, especially with culturally and linguistically different students. But we find that still today too many policies, schools, programs, curricula, and their teachers at all levels are not engaging their students this way. So we must consider: are we complicating our educational problems so much that we fail to see (and accept) the simplicity of possible solutions? Have we finally dehumanized our pedagogy to the point where we have forgotten to find the simplicity in the humanness of educational solutions?

At its core, CAMP is simple. Classes are designed to let students learn together. Mentors and more knowledgeable others are available to the CAMP students to provide personal and academic support. Students work and learn together to build relationships, and to earn one another's trust. Students are placed in courses based on their current academic abilities. Teachers who are invested in student success are part of the CAMP equation. Teachers provide tutoring to help their students learn and understand. Students are provided with access to college with tuition assistance. This last one is key—the students had *access* to a community of practice. The CAMP scholarship provided access to marginalized Mexican-descent students that allowed them to engage in the practice of learning to be a successful student. But is this experience applicable to the experiences of other marginalized and minoritized student groups? I believe so. Marginalization happens in different ways to different students. Marginalization is still a lived experience that prohibits students from fully participating in a community of practice that legitimizes, engages, and empowers toward the goal of learning a successful student identity. So the elements and characteristics of the CAMP program are amenable to local needs and student populations. This framework is adaptable by any school or program because it is a fluid philosophical and pedagogical approach to teaching and learning.

It is apparent that schools and classrooms must contend with sociohistorical, cultural, and socioeconomic aspects of schooling that affect the learning and development of marginalized and other minoritized students today. Despite observations of students living under such conditions that may negatively impact their schooling, educators must assume that all students have some sense of agency. Indeed, many such students overcome life obstacles and thrive

(Bempechat, 1998). But we cannot simply hope that they will do it on their own. It is too much to ask of marginalized children and students who need guidance and support. Students from marginalized lived experiences need access to learning situations where key interactions may occur to fuel their agency and to develop a sense of self as a learner and potentially successful student.

In the various interactions that occur inside and outside of the classroom, Rendón (1994) found long ago in her study of non-traditional college students that faculty, staff, and others "can transform even the most vulnerable students into powerful learners" (p. 46). At the high school level, Conchas (2001) argued that although schools can be sites for maintaining the social and economic status quo, they can just as readily "circumvent inequality if students and teacher work in consort toward academic success" (p. 502). So, in spite of any oppressive institutional, ideological, or curricular forces driving policy or pedagogy in today's schools and educational system, we know great things can emerge from those spaces that create communities that practice the possible. Policy makers and administrators indeed do know this. And we all know that No Child Left Behind has all but stymied the power and potential of what teaching and learning could be. So we can no longer use the stranglehold of NCLB policy as an excuse. Even today, federal policy makers are unsure of how to reconstitute NCLB, recognizing its many shortcomings in pushing for high achievement for all. So, in thinking about what works and what does not in their schools, policy makers, administrators, educators, and parents must understand how the humanizing aspect of teaching and learning is essential for our students today. And the intimate communities that practice this pedagogy, in spaces where there are key interactions, perhaps can get students to begin to see how learning matters to them, and that they matter to schools.

By providing a community in which agency can be nurtured and students can be placed on a trajectory toward learning, being, and becoming, there is the chance that students will be able to thrive on their own. And they will indeed learn something. It is not known whether the student will succeed or fail. But the educator still creates a pedagogy of hope and possibility by letting the students be there in that effort, and to try. We must at least let them try.

# Bibliography

ACT Educational Services. (2008). *National collegiate retention and persistence to degree rates*. Iowa City, IA: ACT Inc.

Allen, J. P., Philliber, S., Herrling, S., and Kuperminc, G. P. (1997). Preventing teen pregnancy and academic failure: Experimental evaluation of a developmentally based approach. *Child Development, 68*(4), 729–742.

Anzaldúa, G. (1999). *Borderlands/La frontera: The new mestiza*. San Francisco, CA: Aunt Lute Books.

Auerbach, S. (2006). "If the student is good, let him fly": Moral support for college among Latino immigrant parents. *Journal of Latinos and Education, 5*(4), 275–292.

Barajas, H. L., and Pierce, J. L. (2001). The significance of race and gender in school success among Latinas and Latinos in college. *Gender and Society, 15*(6), 859–878.

Bartlett, L., and D. Holland. (2002). Theorizing the space of literacy practices. *Ways of Knowing, 2*(1) 10–22.

Bartolomé, L. I. (1994). Beyond the methods fetish: Toward a humanizing pedagogy. *Harvard Educational Review, 64*(2), 173–194.

Barton, D., and Tusting, K. (2005). *Beyond communities of practice: Language, power and social context*. Cambridge: Cambridge University Press.

Bempechat, J. (1998). *Against the odds: How "at-risk" children exceed expectations*. San Francisco, CA: Jossey-Bass.

Bettinger, E. P., and Long, B. T. (2009). Addressing the needs of under-prepared students in higher education: Does college remediation work? *Journal of Human Resources, 44*(3), 736–771.

Bourdieu, P. (1990). *The logic of practice*. Stanford, CA: Stanford University Press.

Britzman, D. (1998). *Lost subjects, contested objects: Toward a psychoanalytic inquiry of learning*. Albany, NY: SUNY Press.

Brooks, J. H., and DuBois, D. L. (1995). Individual and environmental predictors of adjustment during the first year of college. *Journal of College Student Development, 36*(4), 347–360.

Campa, B. (2010). Critical resilience, schooling processes, and the academic success of Mexican Americans in a community college. *Hispanic Journal of Behavioral Sciences, 32*(3), 429–455.

Campos, C. M. T., Phinney, J. S., Perez-Brena, N., Chami, K., Ornelas, B., Nemanim, L., . . . Ramirez, C. (2009). A mentor-based targeted intervention for high-risk Latino college freshmen: A pilot study. *Journal of Hispanic Higher Education, 8*(2), 158–178.

Cárdenas, J. (1995). *Multicultural education: A generation of advocacy.* Needham Heights, MA: Simon and Schuster Custom Publishing.

Ceja, M. (2004). Chicana college aspirations and the role of parents: Developing educational resiliency. *Journal of Hispanic Higher Education, 3*(4), 338–362.

Clandinin, D., and Connelly, F. (2000). *Narrative inquiry: Experience and story in qualitative research.* San Francisco, CA: Jossey-Bass.

Conchas, G. Q. (2001). Structuring failure and success: Understanding the variability in Latino school engagement. *Harvard Educational Review, 71*(3), 475–504.

Creswell, J. W. (2007). *Qualitative inquiry and research design: Choosing among five approaches* (2nd ed.). Thousand Oaks, CA: Sage.

Cummins, J. (1996). *Negotiating identities: Education for empowerment in a diverse society.* Ontario, CA: California Association for Bilingual Education.

Cummins, J. (2000). *Language, power, and pedagogy: Bilingual children in the crossfire.* Buffalo, NY: Multilingual Matters.

Darder, A. (1991). *Culture and power in the classroom: A critical foundation for bicultural education.* Westport, CT: Bergin and Garvey.

Donato, R. (1997). *The other struggle for equal schools: Mexican Americans during the civil rights era.* Albany, NY: State University of New York Press.

Faltis, C. J., and Arias, M. B. (1993). Speakers of languages other than English in the secondary school: Accomplishments and struggles. *Peabody Journal of Education, 69,* 6–29.

Faltis, C. J., and Arias, B. (2007). Coming out of the ESL ghetto: Promising practices for Latino immigrant students and English learners in hypersegregated secondary schools. *Journal of Border Educational Research, 6*(2), 19–35.

Fashola, O. S., and Slavin, R. E. (2001). Effective dropout prevention and college attendance programs for Latino students. In R. E. Slavin and M. Calderón (Eds.) *Effective programs for Latino students* (pp. 67–100). Mahwah, NJ: Lawrence Erlbaum Associates.

Fránquiz, M. E., and Salazar, M. del Carmen. (2004). The transformative potential of humanizing pedagogy: Addressing the diverse needs of Chicano/Mexicano students. *High School Journal, 87*(4), 36–53.

Freire, P. (1970). *Pedagogy of the oppressed.* New York, NY: Continuum.

Freire, P. (2004). *Pedagogy of hope.* New York, NY: Continuum.

Fry, R. (2002). *Latinos in higher education: Many enroll, too few graduate*. Washington, DC: Pew Hispanic Center.

Fry, R. (2004). *Latino youth finishing college: The role of selective pathways*. Washington, DC: Pew Hispanic Center.

Fry, R. (2011). *Hispanic college enrollment spikes, narrowing gaps with other groups*. Washington, DC: Pew Hispanic Center.

Gándara, P. (1995). *Over the ivy walls: The educational mobility of low-income Chicanos*. Albany, NY: State University of New York Press.

Gándara, P. (1999). Staying in the race: The challenge for Chicanos/as in higher education. In J. F. Moreno (Ed.), *The elusive quest for equality: 150 years of Chicano/Chicana education* (pp. 169–196). Cambridge, MA: Harvard Educational Review.

Gándara, P. (2002). A study of High School Puente: What we have learned about preparing Latino youth for postsecondary education. *Educational Policy, 16*(4), 474–495.

Gándara, P., and Contreras, F. (2009). *The Latino education crisis: The consequences of failed social policies*. Cambridge, MA: Harvard University Press.

Gándara, P., O'Hara, S., and Gutiérrez, D. (2004). The changing shape of aspirations: Peer influence on achievement behavior. In M. Gibson, P. Gándara, and J. P. Koyama (Eds.), *School connections: U.S. Mexican youth, peers, and school achievement* (pp. 39–62). New York, NY: Teachers College Press.

Garcia, E. (2001). *Hispanic education in the United States: Raíces y alas*. Boulder, CO: Rowman and Littlefield.

Gay, G. (2000). *Culturally responsive teaching: Theory, research, and practice*. New York, NY: Teachers College Press.

Gibson, M. A. (2005). It's all about relationships: Growing a community of college-oriented migrant youth. In L. Pease-Alvarez and S. R. Schecter (Eds.), *Learning, teaching, and community: Contributions of situation and participatory approaches to educational innovation* (pp. 47–68). Mahwah, NJ: Lawrence Erlbaum Associates.

Gibson, M. A., Bejínez, L. F., Hidalgo, N., and Rolón, C. (2004). Belonging and school participation: Lessons from a migrant student club. In M. A. Gibson, P. Gándara, and J. P. Koyama (Eds.), *School connections: U.S. Mexican youth, peers, and school achievement* (pp. 129–149). New York, NY: Teachers College Press.

Gibson, M. A., Gándara, P., and Koyama, J. P. (2004). The role of peers in the schooling of U.S. Mexican youth. In M. A. Gibson, P. Gándara, and J. P. Koyama (Eds.), *School connections: U.S. Mexican youth, peers, and school achievement* (pp. 1–17). New York, NY: Teachers College Press.

Gibson, M. A., and Ogbu, J. U. (1991). *Minority status and schooling: A comparative study of immigrant and involuntary minorities*. New York, NY: Garland.

Gloria, A. M., Castellanos, J., and Orozco, V. (2005). Perceived educational barriers, cultural fit, coping responses, and psychological well-being of Latina undergraduates. *Hispanic Journal of Behavioral Sciences, 27*(2), 161–183.

González, K. P., Jovel, J. E., and Stoner, C. (2004). Latinas: The new Latino majority in college. *New Directions for Student Services, 105,* 17–27.

González, K. P., Stoner, C., and Jovel, J. E. (2003). Examining the role of social capital in access to college for Latinas: Toward a college opportunity framework. *Journal of Hispanic Higher Education, 2*(1), 146–170.

Green, P. E. (2003). The undocumented: Educating the children of migrant workers in America. *Bilingual Research Journal, 27*(1), 51–71.

Greene, J., and Forster, G. (2003). *Public high school graduation and college readiness rates in the United States.* Education Working Paper no. 3. September. New York, NY: Manhattan Institute, Center for Civic Information.

Gudiño, O. G., and Lau, A. S. (2010). Parental cultural orientation, shyness, and anxiety in Hispanic children: An exploratory study. *Journal of Applied Developmental Psychology, 31,* 202–210.

Harris, S. R., and Shelswell, N. (2005). Moving beyond communities of practice in adult basic education. In D. Barton and K. Tusting (Eds.) *Beyond communities of practice: Language, power, and social context* (pp. 158–179). New York, NY: Cambridge University Press.

Hirsch, J. S. (2003). *A courtship after marriage: Sexuality and love in Mexican transnational families.* Berkeley, CA: University of California Press.

Hoffman, S. D. (2006). *By the numbers: The public costs of adolescent childbearing.* Washington, DC: National Campaign to Prevent Teen Pregnancy.

Holland, D., and Eisenhart, M. (1990). *Educated in romance: Women, achievement, and college culture.* Chicago, IL: University of Chicago Press.

Holland, D., Lachicotte, W., Skinner, D., and Cain, C. (1998). *Identity and agency in cultural worlds.* Cambridge, MA: Harvard University Press.

Hondagneu-Sotelo, P. (1992). Overcoming patriarchal constraints: The reconstruction of gender relations among Mexican immigrant women and men. *Gender and Society, 6*(3), 393–415.

Hurtado, S. (2002). Creating a climate of inclusion: Understanding Latino/a college students. In W. A. Smith, P. G. Altbach, and K. Lomotey (Eds.), *The racial crisis in American higher education: Continuing challenges for the twenty-first century* (pp. 121–135). Albany, NY: State University of New York Press.

Jiménez, K. P. (2005). Lengua latina: Latina Canadians (re)constructing identity through a community of practice. In L. Pease-Alvarez and S. R. Schecter (Eds.), *Learning, teaching, and community: Contributions of situated and participatory approaches to educational innovation* (pp. 235–256). Mahwah, NJ: Lawrence Erlbaum Associates.

Josselson, R. (1994). The theory of identity development and the question of intervention: An introduction. In S. L. Archer (Ed.), *Interventions for adolescent identity development* (pp. 12–25). Thousand Oaks, CA: Sage.

Kirst, M., and Venezia, A. (2001). Bridging the great divide between secondary schools and postsecondary education. *Phi Delta Kappan, 83*(1), 92–97.

Koyama, J., and Gibson, M. A. (2007). Marginalization and membership. In J.A. Van Galen and G. W. Noblit (Eds.), *Late to class: Social class and schooling in the new economy* (pp. 87–111). Albany, NY: SUNY Press.

Lave, J., and Wenger, E. (1991). *Situated learning: Legitimate peripheral participation*. Cambridge: Cambridge University Press.

Lea, M. R. (2005). "Communities of practice" in higher education: Useful heuristic or educational model? In D. Barton and K. Tusting (Eds.), *Beyond communities of practice: Language, power and social context* (pp. 180–197). Cambridge: Cambridge University Press.

Leyendecker, B., Harwood, R. L., Lamb, M. E., and Schölmerich, A. (2002). Mothers' socialisation goals and evaluations of desirable and undesirable everyday situations in two diverse cultural groups. *International Journal of Behavioral Development, 26*, 248–258.

Macedo, D. (1994). *Literacies of power: What Americans are not allowed to know*. Boulder, CO: Westview Press.

Matute-Bianchi, M. E. (1991). Situational ethnicity and patterns of school performance among immigrant and nonimmigrant Mexican-descent students. In M. A. Gibson and J. U. Ogbu (Eds.), *Minority status and schooling: A comparative study of immigrant and involuntary minorities* (pp. 205–247). New York: Garland.

Matute-Bianchi, M. E. (2008). Situational ethnicity and patterns of school performance among immigrant and nonimmigrant Mexican-descent students. In J. U. Ogbu (Ed.), *Minority status, oppositional culture, and schooling* (pp.397–432). New York, NY: Routledge.

McCarthy, M. M., and Kuh, G. D. (2006). Are students ready for college? What student engagement data say. *Phi Delta Kappan, 87*(9), 664–69.

McHatton, P. A., Zalaquett, C. P., and Cranson-Gingras, A. (2006). Achieving success: Perceptions of students from migrant farmwork families. *American Secondary Education, 34*(2), 25–39.

McMillan, J. H., and Reed, D. F. (1994). At-risk students and resiliency: Factors contributing to academic success. *Clearing House, 67*(3), 137–140.

Merriam, S. B. (1988). *Case study research in education: A qualitative approach*. San Francisco, CA: Jossey-Bass.

Merriam, S. B. (1998). *Qualitative research and case study applications in education*. San Francisco, CA: Jossey-Bass.

Mendiola, I. D., Watt, K. M., and Huerta, J. (2010). The impact of Advancement Via Individual Determination (AVID) on Mexican American students enrolled in a 4-year university. *Journal of Hispanic Higher Education, 9*(3), 209–220.

Mora, P. (1993). *Nepantla: Essays from the land in the middle*. Albuquerque, NM: University of New Mexico Press.

Morales, A., and Hanson, W. E. (2005). Language brokering: An integrative review of the literature. *Hispanic Journal of Behavioral Sciences, 27*, 471–503.

Moreno, J. F. (Ed.) (1999). *The elusive quest for equality: 150 years of Chicano/Chicana education*. Cambridge, MA: Harvard Educational Review.

National Center for Education Statistics. (2011). *The condition of education 2011*. NCES 2011 033. May. Washington, DC: National Center for Education Statistics. Retrieved from http://nces.ed.gov/pubsearch/pubsinfo .asp?pubid=2011033.

Noddings, N. (1992). *The challenge to care in schools: An alternative approach to education*. Philadelphia, PA: Falmer.

Ogbu, J. U., and Simons, H. D. (1998). Voluntary and involuntary minorities: A cultural–ecological theory of school performance with some implications for education. *Anthropology and Education Quarterly, 29*(2), 155–188.

Olsen, L., and Jaramillo, A. (1999). *Turning the tides of exclusion: A guide for educators and advocates for immigrant students*. Oakland, CA: California Tomorrow.

Orfield, G., and Lee, C. (2005). *Why segregation matters: Poverty and educational inequality*. Cambridge, MA: Civil Rights Project, Harvard University.

Oseguera, L., Locks, A. M., and Vega, I. I. (2009). Increasing Latina/o students' baccalaureate attainment: A focus on retention. *Journal of Hispanic Higher Education, 8*(1), 23–53.

Osterman, K. F. (2000). Students' need for belonging in the school community. *Review of Educational Research, 70*(3), 323–367.

Pascarella, E. T., and Terenzini, P. T. (1991). *How college affects students: Findings and insights from twenty years of research*. San Francisco, CA: Jossey-Bass.

Pascarella, E. T., and Terenzini, P. T. (2005). *How college affects students: A third decade of research*. San Francisco, CA: Jossey-Bass.

Rendón, L. (1994). Validating Culturally Diverse Students: Toward a New Model of Learning and Student Development. *Innovative Higher Education, 19*(1), 33–51.

Reyes, M. (1992). Challenging venerable assumptions: Literacy instruction for linguistically different students. *Harvard Educational Review, 62,* 427–446.

Reyes, R, III. (2006). Cholo to "me": From peripherality to practicing student success for a Chicano former gang member. *Urban Review, 38*(2), 165–186.

Reyes, R., III. (2007). A collective pursuit of learning the possibility to be: The CAMP experience assisting situationally marginalized Mexican American students to a successful student identity. *Journal of Advanced Academics, 18*(4), 618–659.

Reyes, R., III. (2009). "Key interactions" as agency and empowerment: Providing a sense of the possible to marginalized, Mexican-descent students. *Journal of Latinos and Education, 8*(2), 105–118.

Romo, H., and Falbo, T. (1996). *Latino high school graduation: Defying the odds*. Austin: University of Texas Press.

Rose, M. (2005). *Lives on the boundary: The struggles and achievements of America's underprepared*. New York, NY: Free Press.

Rose, M. (2006). *Possible lives: The promise of public education in America*. New York, NY: Penguin Books.

Salerno, A. (1991). *Migrant students who leave school early: Strategies for retrieval*. Charleston, WV: ERIC Clearinghouse on Rural Education and Small Schools. (ERIC Document Reproduction Service No. ED437228)

Salinas, C., and Reyes, R. (2004). Creating successful academic programs for Chicana/o high school migrant students: The role of advocate educators. *High School Journal, 87*(4), 54–66.

Schultz, K. (2001). Constructing failure, narrating success: Rethinking the "problem" of teen pregnancy. *Teachers College Record, 103*(4), 582–607.

Schutte, O. (1993). *Cultural identity and social liberation in Latin American thought*. Albany, NY: State University of New York Press.

Slavin, R. E., and Calderón, M. (Eds.) (2001). *Effective programs for Latino students*. Mahwah, NJ: Lawrence Erlbaum Associates.

Stake, R. (1995). *The art of case study research*. Thousand Oaks, CA: Sage.

Stanton-Salazar, R. D. (1997). A social capital framework for understanding the socialization of racial minority children and youths. *Harvard Educational Review, 67*, 1–40.

Stanton-Salazar, R. D. (2001). *Manufacturing hope and despair: The school and kin support networks of U.S.-Mexican youth*. New York, NY: Teachers College Press.

Sy, S. R. (2006). Family and work influences on the transition to college among Latina adolescents. *Hispanic Journal of Behavioral Sciences, 28*(3), 368–386.

Tinto, V. (1993). *Leaving college: Rethinking the causes and cures of student attrition*. Chicago, IL: University of Chicago Press.

Trueba, H. (1989). *Raising silent voices: Educating the linguistic minorities for the 21st century*. New York: Newbury House.

Trueba, H. (2002). Multiple ethnic, racial, and cultural identities in action: From marginality to a new cultural capital in modern society. *Journal of Latinos and Education, 1*(1), 7–28.

Tse, L. (1995). Language brokering among Latino adolescents: Prevalence, attitudes, and school performance. *Hispanic Journal of Behavioral Sciences, 17*(2), 180–193.

Urrieta, Jr., L. (2009). *Working from within: Chicana and Chicano activist educators in whitestream schools*. Tucson, AZ: University of Arizona Press.

US Department of Education. (2005). *HEP/CAMP Grantee Performance Report*. Washington, DC: U.S. Department of Education.

Valadez, J. R. (1996). Educational access and social mobility in a rural community college. *Review of Higher Education, 19*(4), 391–409.

Valdés, G. (1996). *Con respeto: Bridging the distances between culturally diverse families and schools*. New York, NY: Teachers College Press.

Valencia, R. R. (1997). *The evolution of deficit thinking: Educational thought and practice*. Washington, DC: Falmer Press.

Valencia, R. R. (Ed.). (2002). *Chicano school failure and success: Past, present and future*. New York, NY: Routledge.

Valencia, R. R., and Black, M. S. (2002). "Mexican Americans don't value education!"—On the basis of the myth, mythmaking, and debunking. *Journal of Latinos and Education, 1*(2), 81–103.

Valencia, R. R., Menchaca, M., and Donato, R. (2002). Segregation, desegregation, and integration of Chicano students: Old and new realities. In R. R. Valencia (Ed.), *Chicano school failure and success: Past, present and future* (pp. 70–113). New York, NY: Routledge.

Valenzuela, A. (1999). *Subtractive schooling: U.S. Mexican youth and the politics of caring*. New York, NY: SUNY Press.

Varenne, H., and McDermott, R. (1998). *Successful failure: The school America builds*. Boulder, CO: Westview Press.

Venezia, A., and Kirst, M. W. (2005). Inequitable opportunities: How current education systems and policies undermine the chances for student persistence and success in college. *Educational Policy, 19*, 283–307.

Vigil, J. D. (1988). *Barrio gangs: Street life and identity in Southern California*. Austin, TX: University of Texas Press.

Vigil, J. D. (2003). Urban violence and street gangs. *Annual Review of Anthropology, 32*(1), 225–232.

Villenas, S., and Moreno, M. (2001). To *valerse por si misma* between race, capitalism, and patriarchy: Chicana mother–daughter pedagogies in North Carolina. *Qualitative Studies in Education, 14*(5), 671–687.

Vygotsky, L. (1978). *Mind in society: The development of higher psychological processes*. Ed. M. Cole, V. John-Steiner, S. Scribner, and E. Souberman. Cambridge, MA: Harvard University Press.

Weis, L. (2008). "Excellence" and student class, race, and gender cultures. In J. U. Ogbu (Ed.), *Minority status, oppositional culture, and schooling* (pp. 240–256) New York, NY: Routledge.

Wenger, E. (1998). *Communities of practice: Learning, meaning, and identity*. Cambridge: Cambridge University Press.

Willison, S., and Jang, B. S. (2009). Are federal dollars bearing fruit? An analysis of the College Assistance Migrant Program. *Journal of Hispanic Higher Education, 8*(3), 247–262.

Wilson, H., and Huntington, A. (2006). Deviant (m)others: The construction of teenage motherhood in contemporary discourse. *Journal of Social Policy, 35*, 59–76.

Winn, P. (2006). *Americas: The changing face of Latin America and the Caribbean*. Berkeley: University of California Press.

Zachry, E. M. (2005). Getting my education: Teen mothers' experiences in school before and after motherhood. *Teachers College Record, 107*(12), 2566–2598.

Zarate, M. E., and Gallimore, R. (2005). Gender differences in factors leading to college enrollment: A longitudinal analysis of Latina and Latino students. *Harvard Educational Review, 75*(4), 383–408.

Zell, M. C. (2010). Achieving a college education: The psychological experiences of Latina/o community college students. *Journal of Hispanic Higher Education, 9*(2), 167–186.

# Source Credits

Portions of chapters 2, 3, and 6 appeared in "Cholo to 'Me': From Peripherality to Practicing Student Success for a Chicano Former Gang Member," *The Urban Review*. Reproduced by permission of Springer.

Portions of chapter 4 appeared in "'Key Interactions' as Agency and Empowerment: Providing a Sense of the Possible to Marginalized, Mexican-Descent Students," *Journal of Latinos and Education* 2009, vol. 8, no. 2. Reprinted by permission of Taylor & Francis Ltd., http://www.tandf.co.uk/journals).

Portions of chapter 7 were previously published in "Potential Almost Lost: A Chicana's Story from the Margins in Her First Year of College," *Latino Studies* 2011, vol. 9, no. 2/3, pp. 336–343. Reproduced by permission of Palgrave Macmillan.

Portions of chapters 2, 3, 5, and 6 were previously published in "A Collective Pursuit of Learning the Possibility to Be: The CAMP Program Assisting Situationally Marginalized Mexican-American Students to a Successful Student Identity," *Journal of Advanced Academics* 2007, vol. 18, no. 4, pp. 618–659.

Portions of chapters 2 and 6 were previously published in Reyes III, R., Valles, E., and Salinas, C. "The evolution of Luz: A case study of gendered tensions of romance and domesticity in the life of a former migrant, Chicana college student," *Journal of Hispanic Higher Education* 2011, vol. 10, no. 2, pp. 147–160.

Portions of chapter 3 were previously published in "Struggle, Practice, and Possibility: Lessons Learned from Marginalized Women of Mexican Descent in Their First Year of College through the CAMP Program," *Equity and Excellence in Education* 2007, vol. 40, no. 3, pp. 218–28.

# Index

# About the Author

Reynaldo Reyes is Associate Professor of teacher education in the College of Education at the University of Texas at El Paso. His research focuses on issues of identity and how learning and life experiences impact the schooling experiences of marginalized student populations, especially English-language learners and Latino student populations, at the secondary and postsecondary levels. His current research is looking at the role(s) that the AVID (Advancement Via Individual Determination) program for English learners plays in identity and strategies in learning language and content and making the students college-ready. Finally, he also does work in migrant education in which he explores how schools can best meet their personal, linguistic, and educational needs.

His work has been published in numerous academic journals, including the *Urban Review, Equity and Excellence in Education,* and the *Journal of Latinos and Education,* among others. Reynaldo Reyes was also guest editor of a special issue of the *Journal of Border Educational Research* (out of Texas A&M International University) titled *Marginalized Students in Secondary School Settings: The Pedagogical and Theoretical Implications of Addressing the Needs of Student Sub-Populations.* He recently completed a Fulbright Scholar Award in Fall 2012 at Pontificia Universidad Católica de Chile in Santiago.